Secretaries of War
and
Secretaries of the Army

SECRETARIES
OF WAR
AND
SECRETARIES
OF THE ARMY

Portraits & Biographical Sketches

by

William Gardner Bell

CENTER OF MILITARY HISTORY
UNITED STATES ARMY
WASHINGTON, D.C., 1992

Library of Congress Cataloging in Publication Data

Bell, William Gardner.
    Secretaries of war and secretaries of the army.

    Bibliography: p.
    Includes index.
    1. United States. Dept. of the Army—Officials and employees—Biography. 2. United States. War Dept.—Officials and employees—Biography. 3. Cabinet officers—United States—Biography. I. Title.
E176.B42   353.62'092'2 [B]   80-20122

First Printed 1981—CMH Pub 70–12

For sale by the U.S. Government Printing Office
Superintendent of Documents, Mail Stop: SSOP, Washington, DC 20402-9328
ISBN 0-16-036191-5

FOREWORD

The principle of civilian control over the military dates back to the founding of the nation. Despite the historical acceptance and application of this principle and despite the importance of the Army's civilian leaders in both military and wider national affairs, the Army has lacked a comprehensive catalog of its secretaries.

This book should be useful in connection with presidential nomination of Army secretaries, as a handbook for the Congressional armed services committees, and as a reference work throughout the Army. Students and scholars in such diverse fields as history, political science, American studies, and art and portraiture will find the book of interest. It should also be a unique research and reference tool for governmental, academic, and public libraries, and a work of interest to the general public.

Originally prepared during the bicentennial period, this volume calls the roll of the Secretaries of War and the Secretaries of the Army and honors them for their contributions as eminent leaders in the Army's and the nation's history.

Washington, D.C.
30 March 1992

HAROLD W. NELSON
Brigadier General, USA
Chief of Military History

THE AUTHOR

William Gardner Bell was inducted into the Army in 1941, was commissioned through the officer candidate course at the Cavalry School in 1943, and served in the Italian Campaign in 1944–1945 as a platoon leader, company commander, and battalion staff officer with the 350th Infantry Regiment, 88th Infantry Division. From 1947 to 1950 he was associate editor of the *Cavalry Journal,* and from 1950 to 1953, as editor of *Armor Magazine,* he assured that the mounted arm's publication reflected the transition from horse to horsepower. From 1956 to his retirement in 1962 he served as a historian in the Office of the Chief of Military History; in 1963 he returned as a civilian historian. Before embarking upon this book, he compiled the annual reports of the Secretary of the Army and the annual Department of the Army Historical Summary. He served as the staff specialist on the frontier army and wrote the Indian Wars chapter of the Army's historical volume *American Military History.*

PREFACE TO THE FIRST PRINTING

A little over a hundred years ago, against a backdrop of a century of American independence, Secretary of War George Washington McCrary wrote Lurton Dunham Ingersoll, a well-informed and well-connected individual then in charge of the War Department Library, to suggest that Ingersoll prepare a history of the department for publication. Ingersoll adopted the proposal with alacrity, although it would be a private venture, and his book, *A History of the War Department of the United States With Biographical Sketches of the Secretaries,* was published in 1880.

In the opening lines, Ingersoll noted that "in nearly all instances" the War Department had been "placed in the control of men of high renown throughout the republic, and indeed throughout Christendom." He noted further that "in but very few instances had it been given in charge to men of ordinary abilities or of little reputation."

The department's second century, recently completed, is a match for its first, and tends to confirm Ingersoll's assessment, although many of the secretaries would have been quick to disavow the superlatives. The occasion of the bicentennial thus offered a suitable historical moment in which to compile a comprehensive record of the Army's civilian leaders over the course of the two hundred years since the War Office was established.

Although this is the first Army historical publication to be devoted exclusively to the civilian leadership, the department heads have not been ignored previously; the secretarial dimension has been woven into every one of the department's official historical works where its inclusion was germane.

Considerations of style and format have dictated the approach to the biographical feature of this book. Thus the personality sketches, telegraphic in nature, have been scaled roughly to uniform size despite variations in the terms of office, substance of service, and celebrity or distinction of the incumbents. Army stewardship is the common denominator.

It also seemed appropriate to include in the main listing of office holders only the primary secretaries —those nominated by the President and confirmed by the Senate. The only exceptions are James Monroe and James Porter. Monroe, while Secretary of State, a position to which he had been nominated and confirmed, was designated by President James Madison to serve concurrently as Secretary of War following Secretary John Armstrong's resignation, and Monroe ran the War Department for an extended period in wartime. Porter served as secretary for almost a full year before the Senate, for political reasons, declined to confirm him.

A break in continuity in public office is not an unusual thing, of course, and interruptions in secretarial progression have occurred through the years. Secretaries ad interim have been required on a number of occasions. Often they were high level Army officers who carried out the secretarial function in addition to their other duties. These temporary and unconfirmed officials are reviewed in Appendix A.

Published sources disagree on the dates of secretarial incumbency; disparities exist because compilers have used such different service bases as date of appointment, date of announcement, date of acceptance, date of confirmation, date of administration of the oath of office, or date of assumption of office. For purposes of consistency, the dates set out in the Department of the Army Manual, an internal reference handbook published for many years and drawn upon for other publications and uses, have been cited herein and are treated as authoritative.

For readers who wish to probe more deeply into the history of the United States Army, the operation of the departmental headquarters, the lives of the respective secretaries, or the backgrounds of the portrait painters, a selective bibliography is supplied. Intended only as a starting point, it is by no means exhaustive. The material available on the secretaries is as uneven as the careers of the individuals involved. Full biographies, if not autobiographies, exist on the more prominent figures, while little information is available on others of more modest service. The same may be said with even more emphasis where the painters are concerned.

Every effort has been made to ensure that the material in this book is accurate, but because of the two-century time span, a paucity of records, and occasionally conflicting information, it is possible that errors have crept in. There are also some informational gaps, especially on the portrait painters. Corrections, documented where possible, and missing pieces of information such as the date and location of an artist's birth or death, may be addressed to the Chief of Military History, Department of the Army, Washington, D.C. 20314. For readers primarily interested in the paintings reproduced in this work, portrait dimensions are given in inches, with height preceding width, and are sight measurements in the frame.

Thanks are due Mr. John G. Connell, Jr., former Administrative Assistant to the Secretary of the Army, for his interest and assistance in this project. As the pivotal administrative official in the Army civilian secretariat under fifteen department heads ranging from Secretary Stimson to Secretary Alexander, Mr. Connell superintended the secretarial portrait collection with a careful regard for its unique character and its historical significance. Mr. Thomas J. Scheblik and Mr. C. Leslie Walleigh, former directors of the Defense Supply Service, Washington, were also most helpful in their agency's Pentagon custodial role.

The Department of the Army, the Center of Military History, and the author gratefully acknowledge the substantive assistance of key staff members of a number of official and private agencies and institutions: Mrs. Mona Dearborn, Keeper of the Catalog of American Portraits, and Mr. Richard K. Doud, Survey Coordinator, of the National Portrait Gallery; Mrs. Katherine Ratzenberger, Assistant Librarian of the National Collection of Fine Arts and the National Portrait Gallery; Mr. Michael Musick, Archivist in the National Archives; Mr. George Hobart, Curator of Documentary Photography in the Library of Congress; Mrs. Andrea Ericson, Gallery Director, Portraits, Inc., New York; and numerous directors, curators, research assistants, and librarians of museums, galleries, historical societies, and libraries.

The author is indebted to three independent reviewers who read and commented upon the manuscript: Russell F. Weigley, Professor of History at Temple University and a member of the Department of the Army Historical Advisory Committee; Edward M. Coffman, Professor of History at the University of Wisconsin and Visiting Professor (1977–1978) at the United States Military Academy; and John K. Mahon, Professor of History at the University of Florida and Visiting Professor (1977–1978) at the U.S. Army Military History Institute–U.S. Army War College.

The manuscript was also reviewed within the Center of Military History and the author benefited from the comments of key members of the professional staff: Dr. Maurice Matloff, Chief Historian, and Dr. Robert W. Coakley, Deputy Chief Historian; Col. James F. Ransone, Jr., Chief, Histories Division, and Dr. Walter G. Hermes, Chief, Staff Support Branch; Col. William F. Strobridge, Chief, Historical Services Division; and Mrs. Marian R. McNaughton, Staff Art Curator, and Miss Marylou Gjernes, Museum Specialist, Army Art Activity. Mrs. Loretto C. Stevens gave generously of her time and editorial experience from the earliest stages of preparation. Mrs. Anita L. Dyson typed the manuscript, and Mrs. Joanna M. Fringer edited it.

Mr. James M. Breedlove of the Adjutant General Center designed the book. Mr. William Rosenmund and Mrs. Viola Destefano of the Army Audiovisual Activity made important contributions.

A general expression of appreciation must go also to other members of the staff of the U.S Army Center of Military History—historical, reference, editorial, curatorial, clerical, administrative—and the staffs of the National Archives, Library of Congress, General Services Administration, National Portrait Gallery, Defense Supply Service, and Military District of Washington—archivists, librarians, audiovisual and information specialists, photographers, laboratory technicians, administrative force—whose individual contributions always come into focus with the publication of a historical work such as this, but whose recognition is often completely overlooked or submerged under the umbrella credit accorded an institution or the personal mention conferred upon a superior. That it must be that way because of the lines of authority or the rule of numbers neither diminishes the contribution nor dilutes the acknowledgment.

The kind assistance of so many individuals does not relieve the author of full responsibility for the finished work; errors of fact or of interpretation are mine and mine alone.

WILLIAM GARDNER BELL
Washington, D.C.

CONTENTS

Secretaries of the Army

List of
Introductory Illustrations

INTRODUCTION

The United States Army has evolved during more than two hundred years from the assorted volunteer elements of a weak confederation of colonies into the composite and balanced standing force of a leading world power. Its evolution has paralleled the social, economic, political, and geographical development of the nation. In the opening struggle for independence, the middle period of continental expansion, and the modern era of international operations, the Army has played a constant and substantive role in American history. Today the Army acts in concert with the other military services to protect the nation and carry out American policies at home and around the world.

The Army's senior official is its civilian secretary, who conducts its affairs subject only to the direction, authority, and control of the President of the United States as commander in chief and the Secretary of Defense who represents the chief executive as head of the Department of Defense.[1]

The principle of civilian control over the military took root early in colonial America under the stewardship of legislators who, "mindful of classical examples of caesarism and praetorianism, and with the spectacle of Cromwell's military dictatorship arising before them," were determined that such absolute forms of government—especially those of a military complexion—would not gain a foothold in the new land.[2]

As the sentiment for independence came into focus in the closing decades of the eighteenth century, the framers of the Constitution of the United States codified the concept of civil direction over military affairs by assigning to the Congress the power to raise and support armies, make rules for the government and regulation of the land forces, and declare war. In addition the President was given the role of commander in chief of the Army and the Navy and the state militia when called into federal service.

The United States Army was created in June 1775 when the Continental Congress authorized the muster of troops under national auspices and appointed George Washington of Virginia to command them. The Continental Army was administered initially by the Congress, and the creation of an executive military department with carefully defined powers and responsibilities became a lengthy process of trial and error. In June 1776, for example, the Congress established a Board of War and Ordnance composed of five legislators, the lineal ancestor of the War Department. John Adams chaired this congressional committee for more than a year. In July 1777 the Congress established a new Board of War composed first of three and then of five individuals who were not members of Congress. Horatio Gates was named to head it, and served during the winter of 1777–1778.

Further change came in the fall of 1778 when Congress again rearranged the board to consist of two legislators and three outsiders. Timothy Pickering and Richard Peters, two of its members, both signed documents as President during 1779–1780, although neither had been appointed to the office. Then in 1781 the Congress set up a War Office, staffed it with non-legislators, and appointed Benjamin Lincoln to head it with a new title, of British origin, Secretary at War. Henry Knox succeeded him in 1781.

Despite these efforts to provide direction and control over the Army, during the 1780's the Congress often acted upon military matters as a committee of the whole or through special subcommittees, independent of the Board of War and the Secretary at War. Yet there was an unmistakable trend in the direction of a separate military department. All that was needed was the formalization of the executive branch of government and the installation of a chief executive.[3]

On 30 April 1789, George Washington became the first President of the United States under the new Constitution. Three months later, on 7 August 1789, Congress established a Department of War, changed the title of the department head from Secretary *at* War to Secretary *of* War, and made that official directly responsible to the President rather

1

HORATIO GATES (1728–1806), President of the Board of War, 1777–1778. Gates was born in England, served in the British Army under Cornwallis in Nova Scotia, and was wounded at Fort Duquesne in 1755 as a member of Braddock's expedition in the French and Indian War. After further service in the colonies and an interlude in England, he returned to America, embraced the patriot cause, was commissioned in the Continental Army, and served as its adjutant general and an as a field commander in various geographical departments. He retired in 1783 and moved from Virginia to New York in 1790, where he served one term in the state legislature. *Portrait by James Peale after Charles Willson Peale. Oil on canvas, 37 x 29½ inches, ca. 1782. Original in the National Portrait Gallery. The whereabouts of a Gates portrait painted for the Army collection by Daniel Huntington in 1874 is unknown. A texturized photographic reproduction of the Peale portrait hangs in the secretarial gallery.*

than to the Congress. Henry Knox remained in office to become the first Secretary of War.

Another major change in the designation of the department and its executive head came 158 years later with the passage of the National Security Act of 1947. Under this legislation and its 1949 amendments, the Air Force was removed from the Army to become a separate and equal military department, the Army, Navy, and Air Force were brought under a national military establishment headed by a civilian of cabinet rank, and the service secretaries lost cabinet status while their institutions were reduced from executive agencies to military departments within a Department of Defense. The War Department became the Department of the Army, certainly a less bellicose and more precise designation that comprehended its peacetime as well as its wartime role in the military and societal structure. The Secretary of War became the Secretary of the Army, and incumbent Kenneth C. Royall presided over the transition to become the first Secretary of the Army.

In its more than two centuries of service to the nation, the Army has had, by and large, a distinguished body of civilian leaders. A majority of the secretaries studied and practiced law before entering public service. Many moved on to higher public office, and their contributions extended beyond the military sphere. James Monroe and William Howard Taft both achieved the office of President of the United States. John C. Calhoun reached the vice presidency, and Jefferson Davis held a unique office—President of the Confederate States of America.

Nine of the Army's chief executives served also as Secretary of State, three were Secretary of the Treasury, two Postmaster General, and one Attorney General of the United States. William Howard Taft's tenure as Secretary of War was followed by his election to the presidency; he then moved over from the executive to the judicial branch of government to become Chief Justice of the Supreme Court. Another secretary, Edwin M. Stanton, was nominated by President Ulysses S. Grant to be an associate justice of the Supreme Court, but Stanton died before he could take office.[4]

Twenty-one secretaries served in the United States Senate and eighteen in the United States House of Representatives, while nineteen served in state legislatures. Twelve were state governors; one was a territorial governor; and four served as Governor General of the Philippines. Fifteen held diplomatic posts, two were university presidents, and many served at federal and state levels in a variety of other capacities. Henry L. Stimson holds the distinction of being the only one to have served two nonconsecutive terms as Secretary of War, one (1911–1913) under President William Howard

Taft, the other (1940–1945) under President Franklin D. Roosevelt. As the nation entered its third century, Secretary Clifford L. Alexander took office, the first black to head the Army department. Forty of the sixty-nine individuals who have been Secretary of War or Secretary of the Army saw military service, principally in wartime. Jefferson Davis, John M. Schofield, and Howard H. Callaway were graduates of the United States Military Academy, and John W. Weeks was a graduate of the United States Naval Academy. Three other secretaries—Charles M. Conrad, John B. Floyd, and Luke E. Wright—served in the Confederate forces during the Civil War. Michael P. W. Stone served in the British Royal Navy during World War II.

There are two father-son combinations in the roster of Secretaries of War: Simon Cameron (1861–1862) and James D. Cameron (1876–1877); and Alphonso Taft (1876) and William Howard Taft (1904–1908). Another secretary, Robert Todd Lincoln, was the son of a president, and George W. and William H. Crawford were cousins. It is engaging to note that Joel R. Poinsett gave us the lovely Christmas flower, *poinsettia,* while Dwight F. Davis sponsored the Davis Cup, a cherished prize in international tennis competition

The general course of continental development is reflected in the state residency of secretarial appointees (not necessarily their native states). Most early selections came from the New England–Middle Atlantic regions; as settlement spread, there were more nominees from southern and western states. Over the two centuries, New York tops the list with ten appointees. Massachusetts and Pennsylvania are next with six each, while Virginia provided five. Tennessee, Ohio, and Illinois have provided four apiece. Georgia and West Virginia each contributed three of the Army's civilian leaders. Six states—Maryland, South Carolina, Kentucky, Iowa, Michigan, and New Jersey—have had two appointees each, and finally, Louisiana, Minnesota, Vermont, Missouri, Oklahoma, Utah, Kansas, North Carolina, Arkansas, Wisconsin, and California largely confirm the westward trend with one apiece.[5] Secretary Alexander is the first appointee from the District of Columbia.

War Department headquarters has always been located at the seat of government. In the early years of the republic, when the government functioned initially in New York and later in Philadelphia, the department rented modest quarters in private buildings. In New York City, for example, with the Revolutionary War ended and British troops withdrawn, the War Office shared quarters with the Foreign Office in Fraunces Tavern at the corner of Great Dock (now Pearl) and Broad Streets, the site of Washington's farewell address to his officers in 1783. The government's outlay for space to accommodate two of its key, albeit small, departments

BENJAMIN LINCOLN (1733–1810), Secretary at War, 1781–1783. Lincoln was born in Hingham, Massachusetts, and farmed and held local office until trouble with England moved him to higher provincial office and later to Continental military service. Assigned to command the Vermont militia, he served in the north in 1776 and 1777, suffering a serious leg wound at Saratoga. As commander in the south he was forced to surrender Charleston, South Carolina, to the British. Later exchanged, he participated in the Yorktown campaign. In 1787 he led Massachusetts troops that helped suppress Shays's Rebellion, and the next year was a member of the Constitutional Convention. He served a term as lieutenant governor of Massachusetts, held federal office as collector of the port of Boston, and served on several commissions that negotiated treaties with the Indians. *Portrait by James Harvey Young. Oil on canvas, 29 1/4 x 24 1/4 inches, 1874.*

HENRY KNOX (1750–1806), Secretary at War, 1785–1789. Knox was born in Boston of Scotch-Irish parents. His father died when he was twelve, and after working in a Boston bookstore he opened his own London Bookstore there. He was present at the Boston Massacre in 1770, where he tried to restrain British grenadiers from firing on the mob. He joined that city's grenadier corps and studied military science and engineering avidly in his early years. After joining the patriot cause, he organized the American artillery, became an adviser and close friend of General Washington, organized the Continental defenses in several areas, and took part in many Revolutionary battles, including the Delaware crossing. In 1782 he commanded the post at West Point and the following year organized the Society of the Cincinnati. He retired in 1794 to live in Maine. (See also his biographical sketch as first Secretary of War.) *Medallion portrait by Constantino Brumidi, wall of President's Room, Senate Wing, United States Capitol Collection.*

was a modest $812.50 per annum. In May 1788 the offices moved to a house on lower Broadway.[6]

In December 1790, when the federal government moved to Philadelphia, Secretary Henry Knox established his headquarters in Carpenters' Hall, a building the department had occupied while the Confederation Congress was convened in Independence Hall before the move to New York City and the inauguration of constitutional government. The War Department moved in 1791 to adjacent New Hall for a year, then in 1792 to the southeast corner of Fifth and Chestnut Streets in a building that was one of a block of houses called Norris Row. After a four-year residence there, the department moved again in 1797, this time to one of the row houses on the northeast corner of Fifth and Chestnut Streets. Here the headquarters remained until 1800, when the government moved to the new capital at Washington.[7]

Not long after taking office in 1789, President Washington had begun to plan for a new and permanent capital. Throughout most of his tenure he personally attended to the selection of the site, the purchase of the land, the design of the city, and the construction of the public buildings. Only six months after his death in retirement in December 1799, his successor, President John Adams, moved the government to Washington City on the banks of the Potomac River.[8]

George Washington's plan for an executive quarter centered around the President's House had begun to take shape in 1798 with the start of construction on the first two of four similar buildings, to be located on sites about two hundred yards from the corners of the executive mansion. The southeast and southwest structures were completed in 1800, and the War Department occupied space in the southwest unit with several other agencies, while the Treasury Department occupied the southeast unit. Early in their occupancy, both buildings had serious fires that forced the tenants out to rented quarters during a period of reconstruction. The Army headquarters operated on several occasions from private accommodations along the south side of Pennsylvania Avenue between Twenty-first and Twenty-second Streets, a row-house complex sometimes called the Six Buildings.

The government's key departments resumed operations in their rebuilt structures for a dozen years until disaster struck once again during the War of 1812: British forces invaded the capital in 1814 and burned the government buildings to the ground. The War Department again resumed operations in private quarters while the capital was being reconstructed. By 1817 the damaged structures had been rebuilt, and by 1820 the entirely new northeast and northwest buildings had been added

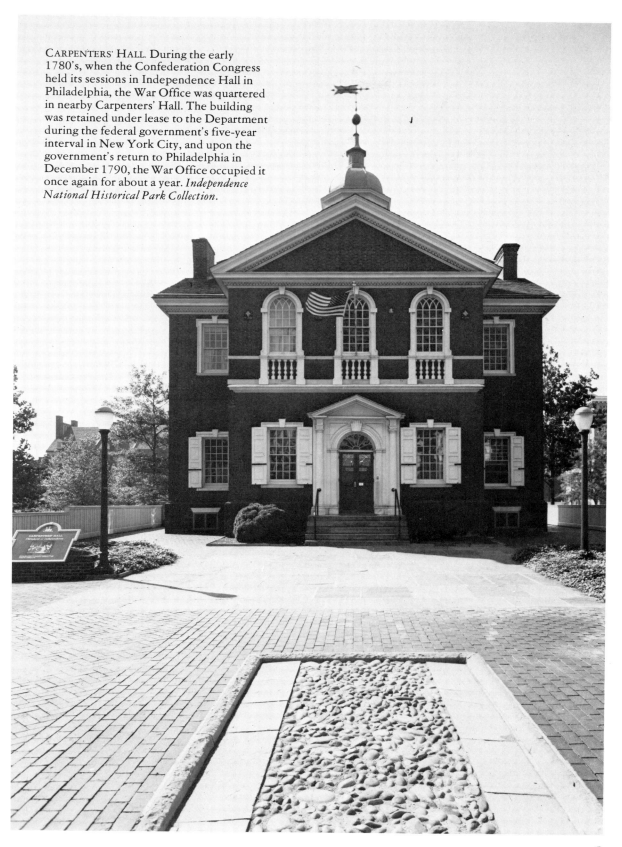

CARPENTERS' HALL. During the early
1780's, when the Confederation Congress
held its sessions in Independence Hall in
Philadelphia, the War Office was quartered
in nearby Carpenters' Hall. The building
was retained under lease to the Department
during the federal government's five-year
interval in New York City, and upon the
government's return to Philadelphia in
December 1790, the War Office occupied it
once again for about a year. *Independence
National Historical Park Collection.*

to the executive grouping. The northeast unit was now occupied by the Department of State, the southeast by the Department of the Treasury, and the southwest by the Department of the Navy. Secretary John C. Calhoun moved the Department of War into the new northwest building, taking along the name War Office for the new edifice, an identification that would later become "Old War."[9]

As the Army's responsibilities were gradually enlarged, the War Department had to expand its staff and facilities to meet both normal growth and the surges created by wartime activity. Because of the expense and delay inherent in new construction, during the Mexican War Secretary William L. Marcy turned to lease arrangements with private builders, while during the Civil War Secretary Edwin M. Stanton secured sufficient funds to add two floors to Old War. Two floors and a wing were added to Old Navy at the same time.[10] Yet, as the years passed it was evident that some major new construction was needed, and the subject was under continuing consideration within the department and elsewhere in the executive and legislative branches of government over an extended period.

In the closing weeks of 1869, the Congress established a commission to select a suitable site and prepare plans for a new executive office building and, in 1871, began annual appropriations for such a structure. Wing-by-wing construction was begun in June 1871 at a site to the west of the White House, near existing northwest and southwest buildings. Progressive demolition of the old

FRAUNCES TAVERN. In the mid-1780's, when the Confederation government was headquartered in New York City, the War Office shared Fraunces Tavern with the Foreign Office. This building, still standing on the corner of Broad and Pearl Streets in lower Manhattan, was the site of General Washington's farewell address to his officers in 1783. *Lithograph by G. Hayward, 120 Water Street, for D. T. Valentine's Manual, 1854. Reproduced from the collections of the Library of Congress.*

buildings was geared to construction of the wings of the new building, and evacuations and occupancies by departmental personnel were carefully phased with construction schedules to ensure optimum use of facilities. The south wing was completed first, in July 1875, and occupied by the State Department. In 1879 the Old War Department building was demolished as the east wing of the new structure was completed, and War and Navy department staff members moved in. Although he had been closely associated, as a department head, with the design, planning, and construction of the State-War-Navy Building, Secretary of War William W. Belknap was not destined to run his department from the new headquarters. That distinction fell to Secretary George W. McCrary, Belknap's successor thrice-removed.

Early in 1888, almost seventeen years after the start of construction, the mammoth State-War-Navy Building was fully completed at a cost slightly greater than $10 million. Under congressional space allocations the War Department initially "occupied all the north, west, and center wings and shared the east wing with the Navy and the south wing with State and Navy."[11]

Expansion of government agencies is a natural concomitant to national growth; as a nation's population and territory grow, political, economic, and social responsibilities multiply, and the various arms of government must expand to keep pace. Agencies seem to constantly outgrow their accommodations, and rarely are the larger departments concentrated in one location or a single building. Fifty years after settling down in the State-War-Navy Building on the west side of the White House grounds, the War Department was being gradually displaced by an expanding State Department and was petitioning for its own building.

Noting that his agencies were occupying seventeen separate buildings throughout the city and that the State Department was scheduled to take over all of State-War-Navy, Secretary George H. Dern in his annual report of 1934 emphasized that "The need for a new War Department building is pressing, and its erection should be undertaken without delay." As if to dramatize the plea, Harry H. Woodring, who as under secretary succeeded Dern upon the latter's death in August 1936, moved the Secretary of War's office out of State-War-Navy and into the Munitions Building on Constitution Avenue, a "temporary" structure left over from World War I. Both the Secretary and the Chief of Staff kept the pressure on, and in his 1938 report, General Malin Craig addressed the subject. Speaking to the demands of efficiency, he emphasized that "A fundamental requisite for the successful conduct of war is that the directing elements of the military machine be closely and mutually

NEW HALL. With the federal government's move from New York back to Philadelphia in December 1790, the War Department resumed operations in its former Carpenters' Hall quarters for about a year. The next move came late in 1791, when the headquarters moved to adjacent New Hall, a new building constructed and owned by the Carpenters' Company. The modest size of the building suggests the modest size of the departmental headquarters in the period. *Independence National Historical Park Collection.*

articulated permitting prompt decisions and their coordinate actions." General Craig warned prophetically that "In the event of a major war one of the first steps that would have to be taken would be the reconcentration of the major elements of the War Department in a single building."[12]

A valid philosophy and an urgent need coincided all too soon as World War II broke out in Europe and the prospect of United States participation loomed ever larger on the horizon. By the end of fiscal year 1941, yet a few months short of American involvement in the war, Secretary Henry L. Stimson, still quartered in the Munitions Building, could report that the space situation had been "somewhat improved by putting into service the New War Department Building on Twenty-first Street, but this was in no way adequate to house all of the personnel." Under emergency conditions, plans for a new building were prepared, a site was selected on the Virginia side of the Potomac River across from the Washington Monument and the Jefferson and Lincoln Memorials, and construction proceeded apace as the nation became ever more deeply involved in the global struggle.[13]

The new building was completed in January 1943, just beyond the midpoint of American participation in the war. Called the "Pentagon" for its

NORRIS ROW. From 1792 to 1796 the War Department was located at the southeast corner of Fifth and Chestnut Streets in one of a group of houses called Norris Row. From 1797 to 1800, when the government moved to Washington, the department was in a similar type of building at the northeast corner of Fifth and Chestnut Streets. *Independence National Historical Park Collection.*

five-sided configuration, the building was constructed at a cost of about $83 million. Secretary Stimson was the first executive to run the department from the new headquarters. By the nation's bicentennial year of 1976, however, although the Pentagon was still the Army's command post, organizational evolution in the military had made the Army a tenant with the other armed services which together constitute the Department of Defense—the Pentagon's proprietor since the parent department was established in 1949.[14]

As the world's largest office building, the Pentagon draws its share of attention in the congeries of public buildings and monuments in the nation's capital. Visitors to its five floors, arranged in five concentric rings and connected by ten corridors radiating from the inner hub, are exposed not only to an architectural marvel but also to a variety of exhibits that represent the military heritage of America. One feature is the Army's "Portrait Gallery" of Secretaries of War and Secretaries of the Army. The gallery represents a unique and valuable collection of paintings of the Army's civilian leaders from earliest times to the present.[15]

Credit for conceiving and launching the gallery belongs to President Grant's Secretary of War, William Worth Belknap. Looking ahead from the vantage point of the early 1870's, Belknap fastened

THE SIX BUILDINGS. Until the executive office buildings that were constructed on the White House grounds were ready for occupancy, the War and Navy Departments were headquartered in what were known as the "Six Buildings," a row of private dwellings on the south side of Pennsylvania Avenue between Twenty-first and Twenty-second Streets in Northwest Washington, just up the street from the executive mansion. These buildings served as alternate accommodations when needed. *Photograph reproduced from the collections of the Columbia Historical Society.*

OLD WAR OFFICE. To create the executive quarter envisioned by President Washington, British architect George Hadfield designed four office buildings that were constructed on the corners of the White House grounds. The southeast and southwest units were erected first and were occupied in 1800. The northeast and northwest units, differing only in the Ionic portico on their Pennsylvania Avenue facade, were opened in 1820. With interruptions from fire and torch, the Department of War occupied the southwest structure, initially called the War Office, from 1800 to 1820, and the northwest unit, later called Old War, from 1820 to 1879, when demolition was begun to make way for construction of the north wing of the State-War-Navy Building. *Drawn by C. Burton, engraved and printed by Fenner, Sears and Company, and published in London in 1831 by L. T. Hinton and Simpkin & Marshall. Reproduced from the collections of the Library of Congress.*

upon the idea of a secretarial portrait gallery as an appropriate way for the department to mark the nation's centennial in 1876. It would not be an easy task; few of his predecessors had had their portraits painted, and even those portraits might be in private possession and out of reach. Thus most of the gallery had to be created from scratch.

For his own portrait, Belknap sat in 1874 for Daniel Huntington, a distinguished portrait, historical, and landscape painter of the day. Most of his predecessors were painted at Belknap's behest during 1873, 1874, and 1875, the bulk of them by three artists who had to work in most instances from existing paintings or family photographs rather than from life. Huntington produced nine, Robert W. Weir—instructor in drawing and professor at West Point—produced seven, and German-born and German-trained Henry Ulke produced five. With the arrival of the centennial year and Belknap's departure from office under a cloud, the War Department Portrait Gallery was a going enterprise that could be updated portrait by portrait by Belknap's successors. This has, indeed, happened.[16]

As the gallery was expanded to cover key officials from a century of operation, it was not limited to secretarial principals alone, but also included

several ad interim secretaries and other officials prominent in the conduct of military affairs. The portraits were executed, in large part, by eminent artists. In addition to Huntington, Weir, and Ulke, they included Walter M. Brackett, a Boston painter and the younger brother of sculptor Edward A. Brackett, who painted Secretaries Pickering, Dexter, Dearborn, and Eustis; George P. A. Healy, a prominent portraitist of statesmen, who painted General William T. Sherman; John Wesley Jarvis, one of the foremost portrait painters of the early nineteenth century in New York, who portrayed Secretary Calhoun; and James Harvey Young, a successful Boston artist, who painted Secretary Henry Knox as well as his predecessor, Secretary at War Benjamin Lincoln. All in all, the quality of the series is commendable when it is remembered that it has been attended by complications, spans a full two hundred years, and is marked by an evolution in both fashion and artistic style.

Because portraiture is a subjective matter involving ego, individuality, and perception as well as creativity, style, and technique, secretarial sitters and painters have not always achieved harmonious results—this despite the fact that the secretaries have traditionally selected their own portraitists. This is not unusual among public figures; in a recent notable instance, Lyndon Baines Johnson

MODIFIED EXECUTIVE OFFICE BUILDING. At Secretary Stanton's direction and with Congressional approval and funding, two floors were added to Old War and Old Navy to meet Civil War expansion requirements. *From Ingersoll's* History of the War Department *(1880), reproduced by the Library of Congress.*

openly expressed his discontent over artist Peter Hurd's portrait of him as the thirty-sixth President of the United States.

Problems related to secretarial portraits occasionally involved not only the subject but also his family. Mrs. Daniel S. Lamont, for example, did not like Raimundo de Madrazo's portrait of Secretary Lamont, and in 1912, seven years after her husband's death, she asked the War Department if it could be exchanged for another. Although the Lamonts had added $2,750 to the War Department's standard $750 fee to retain Madrazo, the portrait had become government property upon submission, and the Judge Advocate General ruled that Congressional action would be required to dispose of it in any manner. The situation was resolved when Mrs. Lamont retained Samantha Huntley to paint a new portrait and presented it to the War Department. Secretary Stimson then acceded to Mrs. Lamont's wishes by hanging the Huntley in the gallery and storing the Madrazo.[17]

The circumstances were somewhat different for Secretary John W. Weeks. He described his portrait as "so satisfactory to my family that they decided they wanted to retain it," so Mr. Weeks arranged for another portrait to represent him in what he noted was sometimes referred to as the "Chamber of Horrors."[18]

The cost of secretarial portraits has risen steadily through the years. Except for the $500 that James

STATE-WAR-NAVY BUILDING. As the nation expanded in the post-Civil War period, governmental departments were enlarged to keep pace and rapidly outgrew their small executive office buildings adjacent to the White House. In 1871 the Congress appropriated funds and construction was begun on a multidepartment building west of the executive mansion. The State-War-Navy Building, erected wing-by-wing, gradually displaced Old War and Old Navy. The War Department was a tenant until 1938. The Executive Office Building, as it is now called, serves today as a White House office annex. *Henri Lovie's perspective drawing of architect Alfred B. Mullett's design. Public Buildings Service reproduction from the National Archives.*

Harvey Young received for his portrait of Henry Knox, the $525 that Henry Ulke received for his portrait of Edwin M. Stanton, the presentation of John Armstrong's portrait, and the transfer from West Point of John C. Calhoun's portrait, the War Department paid $300 for all portraits up to and including Secretary Belknap's. For the portraits of Alphonso Taft through George McCrary, the going rate was $500, while for Robert Lincoln through Russell Alger the portraitist received $750. Elihu Root's portrait by Madrazo cost $2,000, and this departure from scale introduced an element of fluctuation that has existed to this day, with prices ranging from $750 to $2,000 in the earlier years of the twentieth century and increasing to $7,500 in modern times. Artists' fees have been influenced by such factors as the market's trend, the subject's prominence, and the artist's renown.[19]

The Army's secretarial portrait gallery has not functioned in a military vacuum or without surveillance from the art world. In 1931, for example, the members of the American Federation of the Arts, meeting in annual convention and sensitive to the fact that foreign artists like Raimundo de Madrazo and Douglas Chandor were getting the prestigious secretarial commissions, passed a resolution recommending that "all portraits designed for display in a [government] Department building in Washington shall be painted by American artists of recognized standing; that such portraits shall be in oil, of a suitable size, and shall be framed in a simple frame of good design. Also that in each building wall space shall be set apart for the display of portraits, and that a means be taken to bring existing portraits into as much order as may be possible, with regard to size and framing, to the end that the requirements of history, of good order, and of good taste shall be promoted. . . . "[20]

It was perhaps a misnomer to call the War Department's secretarial paintings a "Portrait Gallery" and tie the gallery almost exclusively to the executive portraits, for the Army's total art collection included earlier acquisitions and other categories of work, either commissioned by or purchased for the Army. Through the middle years of the nineteenth century, for example, the Army acquired a series of portraits of Indian chiefs done mostly by Charles Bird King, a series of Mexican War paintings by James Walker, and a series of Civil War etchings by Edwin Forbes. In acquiring these, and other works, the Army demonstrated that, despite organizational and custodial alterations through the years, it perceived the value of art as history and recognized that military art is at once a contribution to the Army's heritage and a tool of morale and esprit.[21]

The thousands of items in the Army Art Collection today represent a variety of regions, periods,

WILLIAM WORTH BELKNAP (1829–1890), Secretary of War, 1861–1876. Shortly after taking office, Belknap conceived the idea of a portrait gallery of the Army's civilian heads as an appropriate way for the department to take note of the nation's centennial in 1876. Engaging the services of such competent artists as Daniel Huntington, Robert Weir, and Henry Ulke, Belknap put them to work painting his long line of predecessors, and he himself sat for Huntington in 1874. Thus the portraits of a century of department heads were painted and assembled in a distinctive collection, continued by Belknap's successors. Despite the stigma attached to his departure from office, Secretary Belknap deserves unqualified credit for the creation of the War Department gallery with its portraits of secretaries and other figures prominent in the conduct of military affairs. (See also his biographical sketch as Secretary of War.) *Photo by Matthew Brady from the Brady Collection in the National Archives.*

and subjects, and constitute a unique body of documentary art. The portraits of the department's secretaries provide substance and foundation in this collection of national as well as military and service significance.[22]

As the United States celebrated its bicentennial in 1976, the specter of inflation was abroad in the land and the high cost of government was a central issue for candidates in the quadrennial presidential election. The new administration had been in office only a few weeks into 1977 when attention turned to the subject of cabinet members' portraits as a possible area of economy.

Three months after taking office, President Jimmy Carter issued a directive to department heads ordering that the custom of commissioning portraits of outgoing agency heads be stopped: "As I understand it, past Cabinet Secretaries have commissioned oil portraits, at Government expense, as a method of maintaining an official, historical record of the line of succession of Cabinet Secretaries. Although the practice has existed for over a century, these portraits have become an unnecessary luxury costing anywhere from $6,000 to

MUNITIONS BUILDING. Edged out of the State-War-Navy Building in the late 1930's by an expanding State Department, the War Department established its next base in the Munitions Building, a World War I temporary structure erected along the Mall on the south side of Constitution Avenue, Northwest, midway between the Washington Monument and the Lincoln Memorial. The Secretary of War maintained his office there until the Pentagon opened in 1943. *Signal Corps photo from the National Archives.*

$12,000. . . . Therefore, I ask that you discontinue this practice and in the future use color photographs to record the line of succession." [23]

President Carter's ban on the commissioning of oil portraits of cabinet secretaries at government expense remained in effect until the eve of his departure from office. As a result of the proscription, the portraits of Carter administration department heads were done in the photographic medium. Assembled in a special exhibit at the National Portrait Gallery in Washington prior to placement in their respective collections, they inspired mixed critical reaction in the nation's press and periodical literature. Whether for this or other reasons, President Carter on 19 January 1981, only twenty-four hours before his departure from office, authorized a return to the traditional custom of contracting for oil portraits to record the line of succession in government departments. Since then the portraits of Secretaries Alexander, Marsh, and Stone have been painted and added to the secretarial portrait gallery in the Pentagon.

It is interesting to note that a bicentennial

NEW WAR DEPARTMENT BUILDING The War Department's sustained appeal through the 1930's for additional construction to ease the space problem was answered with the completion in 1941 of the New War Department Building at Twenty-first Street and Virginia Avenue, Northwest. But the structure was far from the size required to permit a concentration of department offices scattered in various buildings around the District of Columbia and the Virginia suburbs. Although the Under Secretary of War established his office in the new building, the Secretary of War remained in the Munitions Building. *State Department photo.*

PENTAGON. The War Department finally achieved the ideal in spatial accommodations and centralization in January 1943 when it moved across the Potomac River to take up operations in its brand new headquarters—the Pentagon. The world's largest office building, constructed on a plot of swampy wasteland, held space for 30,000 employees. By the end of the World War II decade, however, the Pentagon had evolved from a Department of War to a Department of Defense headquarters, housing elements of all the services. A number of Army offices were moved out to a variety of locations in the Washington metropolitan area. *Navy Department photo from the National Archives.*

appraisal of the Army's secretarial portrait collection placed its value at many times its original cost. Indeed, because of date, subject, or artist, some of the portraits may be said to fall in the category of national treasures.

More than two hundred years ago, George Washington expressed the belief that, "The Instituting of a War Office is certainly an Event of great importance, and, in all probability, will be recorded as such in the Historic page."[24] The first President's observation has been borne out largely because of the efforts of a long line of distinguished secretaries at the head of the department. This book introduces them in consecutive order, with a brief biographical sketch and a portrait of each incumbent.

1. Title 10, United States Code, subtitle B, part I, contains the statutory provisions concerning the organization of the Army and the powers and responsibilities of the secretary.

2. Russell F. Weigley, *History of the United States Army* (New York: Macmillan Co., 1967), p. 6.

3. Maurice Matloff, ed., *American Military History* (Washington: Government Printing Office, 1969), p.55. During gaps in the incumbencies of Gates, Lincoln, and Knox, continuity of operations was ably maintained by Joseph Carlton, who served as administrative assistant in the Board of War and Ordnance, the Board of War, and the Department of War. For a general treatment of the organization and operation of the War Office, see Harry M. Ward, *The Department of War, 1781–1795* (Pittsburgh: University of Pittsburgh Press, 1962).

4. As the nation's third century opened, former Secretary of the Army Cyrus R. Vance was confirmed as Secretary of State in the administration of President Jimmy Carter, becoming the ninth Army secretary to also hold the State portfolio.

5. States are listed in the order in which secretarial candidates from them were appointed. New York receives credit for two appointees for Secretary Stimson's split terms, while North Carolina receives credit for one appointee for Secretary Royall's single term and incumbency during the transition from Secretary of War to Secretary of the Army.

6. Richard S. Patterson, "The [State] Department's New Home—175 Years Ago," *Foreign Service Journal* (Jan 1960):33–31.

7. Ltr, Interior Department, National Park Service, Independence National Historical Park, 29 Apr 77. CMH files.

8. Lurton D. Ingersoll, *A History of the War Department of the United States With Biographical Sketches of the Secretaries* (Washington: Francis B. Mohun, 1880), ch. 4; General Services Administration Historical Study Number 3, *Executive Office Building* (Washington: Government Printing Office, 1970), pp. 2–8; Unpublished "Historical Report of the Executive Office Building," Department of the Interior, 1957, pp. 1–4, CMH files. Although these sources differ on minor details, they are in general accord on the substance of the development of the executive quarter on its present site.

9. GSA Study No. 3, p. 7.

10. To meet emergency housing needs during the Mexican War the government rented two commercial office buildings, one at 17th and F Streets, NW, built by William H. Winder, the other at 15th and F Streets, NW, built by W. W. Corcoran. In the Civil War some badly needed space was acquired by adding two floors to the executive office buildings and a wing to Old Navy. The Winder building was later purchased by the government and remains in use today (1981) as an executive office annex.

11. GSA Study No. 3, p.57; Interior Report, pp. 9–10.

12. Annual Reports of the Secretary of War, 1935, p. 2; 1935, p. 3; and 1938, p. 35. For related details see also the annual reports of 1936, pp. 2, 6, 39; and 1937, pp. 3, 6, 36.

13. Sec'y War Rept, 1941, p. 11. The New War Department Building was turned over to the State Department when Army headquarters moved to the Pentagon; it remains a State Department building today (1981), joined to that agency's new headquarters building constructed on adjacent land in the late 1950's and opened in January 1961.

14. *The Pentagon,* (undated ca. 1943) pamphlet published in Washington, D.C., by the Pentagon Post Restaurant Council. CMH files.

15. In 1992 the portraits of the Secretaries of War were hanging in the inner or "A" Ring on the third floor of the Pentagon between the Fourth and Fifth corridors; those of the smaller number of Secretaries of the Army were in the "A" Ring of the third floor between the Sixth and Seventh corridors. Several of the portraits of key secretaries (Root and Stimson) were hanging in the Secretary of the Army's office, and one—General Knox—was in the General Officers' Mess; texturized photographic reproductions were substituted in the main collection on public display.

16. "Portrait Gallery of Secretary of War Belknap," a list compiled by Dallas Irvine, Chief Archivist, War Records Branch, National Archives, 1955, copy in CMH files. In addition to the predecessors, Huntington painted four and Ulke one of Belknap's successors.

17. Memo, Office of the Assistant and Chief Clerk of the War Department, undated, sub: War Department Portrait Gallery. In Portraits of Ex-Secretaries of War. 007.2, Fine Arts, National Archives.

18 Ltr, John W. Weeks to John C. Scofield, Assistant and Chief Clerk, War Department, 23 Oct 25, sub: Arrangements to provide his portrait for the War Department Gallery. In ibid.

19. Memo, Office of the Assistant and Chief Clerk of the War Deparrment, undated, sub: War Department Portrait Gallery. In ibid.

20. Resolution, The American Federation of the Arts to War Department, 26 May 31, sub: Recommendations concerning portraits of government figures. In ibid.

21. The matter of custodianship surfaces in these examples. Most of the Indian portraits, commissioned by Thomas L. McKenney, first superintendent of Indian Affairs when that bureau was in the War Department, were destroyed by a fire in the Smithsonian Institution in 1865. Fortunately, McKenney had published them privately, in his three-volume work, *History of the Indian Tribes of North America With Biographical Sketches and Anecdotes of the Principal Chiefs* (1836–1844), which perpetuated the gallery and became a classic. Captain Montgomery C. Meigs, an Army engineer officer charged with decorating the Capitol Building, commissioned James Walker to paint "The Battle of Chapul-

tepec" and may have arranged for the acquisition of the twelve small Mexican War and two Civil War paintings by the Army Art Collection. When Edwin Forbes produced his etchings for the nation's centennial celebration, General Sherman took the first set for the Army. They hung in Army offices for many years, apparently gradually disappearing as the headquarters made its frequent moves.

22. The Chief of Military History, who commands the U. S. Army Center of Military History, is custodian of the Army Art Collection. In addition to soldier art and works commissioned with commercial artists, the Center has custody on behalf of the nation of the *Life* and Abbott Laboratories Collections of World War II art. The Army Art Collection includes several watercolors by Adolf Hitler, original cartoons by Bill Mauldin, and important works—in addition to those listed above—by such noted American artists as Peter Hurd, Charles Johnson Post, Norman Rockwell, Howard Brodie, and Tom Lea. Another significant element is a series of portraits of the Army Chiefs of Staff, most of them recently executed through the generosity of former Secretary and Mrs. Robert T. Stevens. These portraits are featured in William Gardner Bell, *Commanding Generals and Chiefs of Staff: Portraits and Biographical Sketches of the United States Army's Senior Officer* (Washington, D.C.: Government Printing Office, 1992). Many pictures from the Army Art Collection are reproduced in Gordon R. Sullivan, *Portrait of an Army* (Washington, D.C.: Government Printing Office, 1991).

23. Memo, President Jimmy Carter, the White House, for Cabinet Officers, 18 Apr 77, directing that the practice of commissioning oil portraits of agency heads be discontinued. Copy in CMH files. News accounts of the period indicate that a constituent of Senator Charles H. Percy of Illinois raised the subject of the cost to the taxpayer of cabinet member portraits. The Illinois legislator was reported to have raised the subject in turn with the director of the Office of Management and Budget; the presidential memorandum followed.

24. George Washington, *The Writings of George Washington* (Washington: Government Printing Office, 1962), vol. 5, p. 159.

Secretaries of War

HENRY KNOX was born in Boston, Massachusetts, on 25 July 1750; upon his father's death left school at twelve to work in a bookstore; joined a local military company at eighteen, was present at the Boston Massacre, 1770, joined the Boston Grenadier Corps in 1772; married Lucy Flucker in 1774; joined the patriot cause and offered his services to General Washington in 1775; was commissioned colonel of the Continental Regiment of Artillery; led the expedition to transfer captured British guns from Fort Ticonderoga to Boston in 1776, a move that forced the British to evacuate the city; led the Delaware River crossing and participated in the Battle of Trenton in 1776; was promoted to brigadier general and Chief of Artillery of the Continental Army, December 1776; participated in the battles of Princeton, Brandywine, and Germantown in 1777 and Monmouth in 1778; sat on the court-martial of Major John Andre in 1780; placed the American artillery at the Yorktown siege in 1781; commanded the West Point post, 1782–1783; organized the Society of the Cincinnati, 1783; was commander in chief of the Army, 23 December 1783–20 June 1784; served under the Confederation as Secretary at War, 8 March 1785–11 September 1789; served under the Constitution as first Secretary of War, 12 September 1789–31 December 1794; prepared a plan for a national militia, advocated and presided over initial moves to establish a regular Navy, urged and initiated the establishment of a chain of coastal fortifications, and supervised Indian policy; retired to Thomaston, Maine, 1796; engaged in lumbering, shipbuilding, stock raising, and brick manufacturing; died in Thomaston on 25 October 1806.

The Artist

James Harvey Young (1830–1918) was born in Salem, Massachusetts and studied architecture before opening a studio in Boston. Examples of his work are in the collections of the American Antiquarian Society and the Essex Institute; the latter organization owns a self-portrait. Young used Gilbert Stuart's painting of Knox, hanging in Faneuil Hall in Boston, to produce a faithful likeness of the Revolutionary War hero, omitting only the cannon Stuart had included as a rest for Knox's left hand, which had been crippled in a hunting accident. Young also painted Benjamin Lincoln for the Army's secretarial portrait gallery.

HENRY KNOX
Washington Administration

By James Harvey Young after Gilbert Stuart
Oil on canvas, 35½" x 28½", 1873

TIMOTHY PICKERING was born in Salem, Massachusetts, on 17 July 1745; graduated from Harvard College, 1763; was commissioned a lieutenant in the Essex County militia, 1766; studied law and was admitted to the bar, 1768; served as judge of the Maritime Court for the Boston-Salem district; wrote *An Easy Plan of Discipline for a Militia* in 1775, one of several guides used by the Army before von Steuben's manual; became colonel of the Essex militia regiment and participated in military operations of the spring of 1775; married Rebecca White, 1776; participated in Revolutionary campaigns in New York and New Jersey; was adjutant general of the Army, 1777–1778, and concurrently a member of the Board of War; was quartermaster general of the Army, 1780–1785; returned to a mercantile business in Philadelphia, 1785; moved to Pennsylvania and organized the county of Luzerne, 1787; served as a delegate to the Constitutional Convention; was appointed by President Washington to treat with the Seneca Indians; was Postmaster General, 1791–1795; was called upon concurrently to negotiate with the Six Nations; served as Secretary of War, 2 January–10 December 1795; advocated establishment of a military academy at West Point and expedited naval ship construction; was Secretary of State ad interim, 20 August–9 December 1795, running the affairs of War and State concurrently; was Secretary of State, 10 December 1795–12 May 1800; returned to farming in Pennsylvania, then Massachusetts; was a Senator from Massachusetts, 1803–1811; was a member of the State Executive Council, 1812–1813; was a Representative from Massachusetts, 1813–1817; died in Salem on 29 January 1829.

The Artist

In the early 1870's, when Secretary Belknap was assembling a War Department gallery, the Army acquired two portraits of Secretary Pickering. One by Walter M. Brackett, painted in 1873, was donated to the United States Military Academy because of Pickering's instrumental role in its founding and remains in the West Point collection today. The other portrait, represented here and hanging in the secretarial gallery in the Pentagon, was painted by an unknown artist at an unknown date and place. A notation in Army records indicates that the Army purchased a Pickering portrait from George E. Daniels of Potter Brothers, New York, who acted on behalf of an unknown owner.

TIMOTHY PICKERING
Washington Administration

By an unknown artist
Oil on canvas, 28¼″ x 23¼″, ca. 1873

JAMES McHENRY was born in Ballymena, County Antrim, Ireland, on 16 November 1753; received a classical education at Dublin University; emigrated to the United States in 1771 followed by his parents a year later; attended Newark Academy in Delaware in 1772; studied medicine in Philadelphia under Dr. Benjamin Rush; joined the patriot cause and volunteered for military service in 1775; was assigned to the military hospital at Cambridge, Massachusetts, as assistant surgeon, 1776; was named surgeon of the 5th Pennsylvania Battalion in August; was captured at Fort Washington in the Long Island campaign in November; was paroled in January 1777 and exchanged in March 1778; was appointed secretary to General Washington in May; was posted to General Lafayette's staff in 1780; was a member of the Maryland Senate from 1781 to 1786 and appointed a delegate to the Confederation Congress in 1783, serving concurrently; married Margaret Allison Caldwell in 1784; was a Maryland delegate to the Constitutional Convention in 1787; was a member of the Maryland commission that welcomed George Washington on his inaugural journey to New York in 1789; served in the Maryland Assembly, 1789–1791; served again in the State Senate, 1791–1795; served as Secretary of War, 27 January 1796–13 May 1800; sustained his predecessor's attention to coastal fortification and naval construction; defended his administration of the department in a formal paper read in the House of Representatives in 1802 and privately printed in 1803; published a Baltimore directory in 1807; served as president of the first bible society founded in Baltimore, 1813; died in Baltimore on 3 May 1816.

The Artist

Although H. Pollock is identified in an early Army portrait list as Miss H. Pollock, an 1873 letter from the artist to Secretary Belknap discloses a masculine hand even though it fails to reveal the writer's sex. Baltimore directories of the period 1868–1886 list a Henry Pollock as a resident of that city at the address on the Belknap letter, and give his occupation as artist and photographer and proprietor of a portrait gallery. This would seem to confirm that Henry Pollock is Secretary McHenry's portraitist. Additional information about him is elusive.

JAMES McHENRY
Washington and J. Adams Administrations

By H. Pollock
Oil on canvas, 29½″ x 24½″, 1873

SAMUEL DEXTER was born in Boston, Massachusetts, on 14 May 1761; studied under the Reverend Aaron Putnam of Pomfret; graduated from Harvard College in 1781; studied law at Worcester under Levi Lincoln, the future attorney general of the United States; was admitted to the bar in 1784; practiced at several locations until settling at Charlestown, Massachusetts, in 1788; married Catherine Gordon that year; served in the state House of Representatives, 1788–1790; served in the U.S. House of Representatives, 1793–1795, and the U.S. Senate, 1799–1800; wrote the memorial eulogy to George Washington upon the first president's death in December 1799; served as Secretary of War, 13 May 1800–31 January 1801; urged congressional action to permit appointment and compensation of field officers for general staff duty; served as Secretary of the Treasury, 1801–1802; briefly conducted the affairs of the Foreign Office and administered the oath of office to Chief Justice John Marshall; returned to private life and the practice of law at Roxbury, Massachusetts; appeared frequently before the higher state courts and the Supreme Court to argue cases; left the Federalist party to espouse Republican views on the War of 1812, opposing an embargo and nonintercourse policy and unsuccessfully contesting its constitutionality; declined a special mission to the Court of Spain tendered by President Madison; was an unsuccessful candidate for governor of Massachusetts in 1814 and 1815; was an ardent supporter of the temperance movement and presided over its first formal organization in his home state; died in Athens, New York, his son's home, on 3 May 1816.

The Artist

Walter M. Brackett (1823–1919) was born in Unity, Maine, the younger brother of sculptor Edward A. Brackett. He spent most of his professional career in Boston, Massachusetts, exhibiting his work at the Boston Athenaeum, the Apollo Association, and the National Academy. He painted the portraits of Secretaries Pickering, Dearborn, and Eustis, in addition to Secretary Dexter's, for the Army's portrait gallery of civilian leaders. His Pickering portrait was donated to West Point.

SAMUEL DEXTER
J. Adams Administration

By Walter M. Brackett
Oil on canvas, 29½″ x 24½″, 1874

HENRY DEARBORN was born in Hampton, New Hampshire, on 23 February 1751; studied medicine under Dr. Hall Jackson at Portsmouth; married Mary Bartlett, his first wife, in 1771; entered practice as a physician in 1772; was elected captain of a militia company; participated in the Battle of Bunker Hill, served under Benedict Arnold in the Quebec expedition and was captured, 1775; was paroled in 1776 and exchanged in 1777; was appointed major of the 3d New Hampshire Regiment; participated in operations at Ticonderoga and Freeman's Farm with the 1st New Hampshire Regiment; spent the winter of 1777–1778 at Valley Forge; took part in the Battle of Monmouth, 1778; engaged in the 1779 operations against the Six Nations; married his second wife, Dorcas Marble, in 1780; joined Washington's staff as deputy quartermaster general; commanded the 1st New Hampshire at Yorktown in 1781; returned to private life in Maine, 1783; was appointed brigadier and major general of militia; was appointed U.S. Marshal for the District of Maine, 1790; served in the U.S. House of Representatives, 1793–1797; served as Secretary of War, 5 March 1801–7 March 1809; helped plan the removal of the Indians beyond the Mississippi; was appointed Collector of the Port of Boston, 1809; was appointed senior major general in the U.S. Army, 1812; was ineffective in command of the northeastern theater in the War of 1812; captured York (Toronto) and Fort George (Quebec) in 1813; was transferred to command in New York City in 1813; married his third wife, Sarah Bowdoin; was nominated and withdrawn for the post of Secretary of War; served as minister to Portugal, 1822–1824; died in Roxbury, Massachusetts, on 6 June 1829.

The Artist

Walter M. Brackett (1823–1919), the Boston artist, became actively engaged in Secretary of War Belknap's plans for an Army portrait gallery, and painted four of the secretary's earliest predecessors — Pickering, Dexter, Dearborn, and Eustis — in 1873. Only Daniel Huntington, Robert W. Weir, and Henry Ulke exceeded his output. Fittingly, his subjects were all residents of Massachusetts. His Pickering portrait is in the West Point collection.

HENRY DEARBORN
Jefferson Administration

By Walter M. Brackett
Oil on canvas, 29½″ x 24½″, 1873

WILLIAM EUSTIS was born in Cambridge, Massachusetts, on 10 June 1753; studied at the Boston Latin School in preparation for college; graduated from Harvard College in 1772; studied medicine under Dr. Joseph Warren; helped care for the wounded at Bunker Hill, where Warren was killed; served in the Revolutionary Army as surgeon of the artillery regiment at Cambridge and then as a hospital surgeon; entered practice in Boston after the war; served as surgeon with the Shays's Rebellion expedition, 1786–1787; became vice president of the Society of the Cincinnati, serving from 1786 to 1810 and again in 1820; served in the Massachusetts legislature (General Court), 1788–1794; was a member of the Governor's Council for two years; served two terms in the U.S. House of Representatives, 1801–1804, having won close races over Josiah Quincy and John Quincy Adams; married Caroline Langdon, 1810; served as Secretary of War, 7 March 1809–13 January 1813; attempted to prepare the Army before the outbreak of the War of 1812, and resigned in the face of criticism following American reverses on the battlefield; was appointed minister to Holland by President Madison, serving from 1814 to 1818; returned home because of ill health; purchased and resided in the historic Shirley Mansion in Roxbury, Massachusetts; was again elected to the U.S. House of Representatives, 1820–1823; ran unsuccessfully for governor of Massachusetts in 1820, 1821, and 1822; was elected governor of Massachusetts and served two terms, 1823–1825; died in Boston while governor, on 6 February 1825.

The Artist

Walter M. Brackett (1823–1919), a Boston artist, painted four Secretaries of War whose stewardship over the department occurred before he was born; indeed, all had died before Brackett reached age seven, which was well before the age of photography and even before Louis Daguerre had perfected his daguerreotype process. Thus Brackett had to rely upon the products of earlier artists and engravers for his image research; he was undoubtedly fortunate that his four subjects were men of both national and regional prominence who were inevitably subjects of pen or brush.

WILLIAM EUSTIS
Madison Administration

By Walter M. Brackett
Oil on canvas, 29½″ x 24½″, 1873

JOHN ARMSTRONG was born in Carlisle, Pennsylvania, on 25 November 1758; interrupted his education at Princeton University when the Revolutionary War broke out, joined the colonial army, and served on the staffs of Generals Mercer and Gates; participated in the Saratoga campaign and was present when Burgoyne surrendered; wrote the famous "Newburgh Letters" in 1783, outlining Continental Army services and grievances; returned to civilian life in Pennsylvania to become secretary of the state's Supreme Executive Council; led state militia into the Wyoming Valley region in 1784 to quell settler disturbances; was appointed state adjutant general of Pennsylvania; was elected a delegate to the Confederation Congress in 1787; married Alida Livingston in 1789; moved to Dutchess County, New York, to settle at Red Hook and engage in agriculture; served in the U.S. Senate, 1800–1802; was reappointed to the Senate to fill De Witt Clinton's unexpired term; was minister to France, 1804–1810; was commissioned a brigadier general and assigned to command New York City and its defenses; served as Secretary of War, 13 January 1813–27 September 1814; was instrumental in securing legislative action for a permanent War Department management staff, and pruned the general officer ranks; shared with President Madison and General William H. Winder the blame for the British capture of Washington and burning of the capital; resigned as secretary in September 1814; returned to agricultural pursuits at Red Hook, New York; wrote *Notices of the War of 1812* (1836) and *A Treatise on Agriculture* (1839); died in Red Hook on 1 April 1843.

The Artist

Daniel Huntington (1816–1906) was born in New York City. He attended Hamilton College in Utica, where Charles Loring Elliott encouraged him to become an artist. He studied under Samuel F. B. Morse and Henry Inman in New York and pursued further studies in Europe, especially in Rome, in the late 1830's and the 1840's, finally achieving a reputation as a leading portrait, historical, and landscape painter. Huntington painted portraits of fifteen Army secretaries, most notably that of William Worth Belknap, creator of the gallery of civilian chief executives. His portrait of Secretary Armstrong, presented to the department by William B. Astor of New York, is after one by John Vanderlyn (1775–1852).

JOHN ARMSTRONG
Madison Administration

By Daniel Huntington after John Vanderlyn
Oil on canvas, 36″ x 29″, 1873

JAMES MONROE was born in Westmoreland County, Virginia, on 28 April 1758; attended private school and entered William and Mary College at sixteen; interrupted his education to become an officer in the Continental Army in 1776; participated in operations at Harlem, White Plains, Trenton, Brandywine, Germantown, and Monmouth; studied law under Governor Thomas Jefferson of Virginia, 1780–1783; served in the Virginia legislature, 1782–1786; served in the Confederation Congress, 1783–1786; married Eliza Kortright, 1786; was admitted to the Virginia bar and practiced at Fredericksburg; was a delegate to the state convention called to ratify the Constitution, 1788; served in the U.S. Senate, 1790–1794; served as minister to France, 1794–1796; was governor of Virginia, 1799–1802; was appointed special envoy to France in 1803 and participated in negotiations related to the Louisiana Purchase; served as minister to Great Britain, 1803–1807; headed a mission to Spain to negotiate American claims to Florida, 1804–1805; was offered and refused the governorship of Upper Louisiana, 1809; was again elected to the Virginia legislature, 1810; was again governor of Virginia, 1811; served as Secretary of State, 1811–1814; served concurrently as Secretary of War, 27 September 1814–2 March 1815; urged that conscription be introduced; was again Secretary of State, 1815–1817; was President of the United States, 1817–1825; enunciated the Monroe Doctrine restraining European intrusions into the Americas; was elected to and presided over the Virginia Constitutional Convention of 1829; moved to New York City after his wife's death to live with his married daughter; died there on 4 July 1831.

The Artist

Robert Walter Weir (1803–1889) was born in New York City. He studied under John Wesley Jarvis and the English heraldic artist, Robert Cox. Weir established himself as a professional artist and studied in Florence, Italy, for three years before opening a New York studio in the late 1820's. In 1834 he became instructor in drawing at the United States Military Academy and was made professor in 1846, a post he held for three decades. A portraitist as well as landscape and genre painter, he executed half a dozen likenesses for the Army gallery.

JAMES MONROE
Madison Administration

By Robert Walter Weir
Oil on canvas, 29½″ x 24½″, 1873

WILLIAM HARRIS CRAWFORD was born in Nelson County, Virginia, on 22 February 1772; during his boyhood the family moved to South Carolina and then to Columbia County, Georgia; studied under Dr. Moses Waddel at Carmel Academy in Augusta, 1796–1798; commenced the practice of law in Oglethorpe County, 1799, and in 1802 completed a digest of the laws of Georgia covering the period 1755–1800; killed Peter L. Van Allen in a duel inspired by political rivalries, 1802; served in the Georgia legislature, 1803–1807; married Sussana Girardin, 1804; suffered a crippled left wrist in a duel with John Clark, 1806; was elected to the U.S. Senate to fill the vacancy created by the death of Senator Abraham Baldwin, 1807; was again elected to the U.S. Senate, 1811, and elected president *pro tempore* upon the death of Vice President George Clinton, 1812; declined an offer to be Secretary of War, 1813; served as minister to France, 1813–1815; served as Secretary of War, 1 August 1815–22 October 1816; recommended to Congress the perpetuation of a War Department management staff; was actively considered by the Republicans as a candidate for president; served as Secretary of the Treasury, 1816–1825, was again a strong candidate for president in 1824; was stricken with paralysis during the campaign and temporarily incapacitated; declined to remain in the John Quincy Adams administration as Secretary of the Treasury; was appointed judge of the Northern Court of Georgia upon the death of the incumbent, 1827; was reelected to the judgeship in 1828 and 1831; died at a friend's home near Elberton, Georgia, while on the judicial circuit, 15 September 1834.

The Artist

Daniel Huntington (1816–1906) of New York was one of the more prolific artists engaged by Secretary Belknap to launch the Army's portrait gallery of civilian leaders. In the period from 1873 to 1876, when the secretarial collection was created and brought up to date, Huntington produced portraits of Horatio Gates, President of the Board of War, and ten of Belknap's predecessors, including Secretary William H. Crawford, as well as Belknap himself. He also painted several interim secretaries, including Generals Grant and Sherman.

WILLIAM HARRIS CRAWFORD
Madison Administration

By Daniel Huntington
Oil on canvas, 29½″ x 24½″, 1875

JOHN CALDWELL CALHOUN was born in Abbeville district, South Carolina, on 18 March 1772; studied under his brother-in-law, Dr. Moses Waddel, at Carmel Academy, Columbia County, Georgia; graduated from Yale College in 1804; studied law at Judge Tapping Reeve's school in Litchfield, Connecticut, and continued his study at Charleston, South Carolina, in the office of Henry W. De Saussure; opened practice at Abbeville in 1807 but gave it up for plantation life; was elected to the South Carolina legislature in 1808 for two terms; married Floride Bouneau Calhoun in 1811; served in the U.S. House of Representatives, 1811–1817; joined the "war hawks" in recommending a declaration of war against England, 1812; served as Secretary of War, 8 October 1817–7 March 1825; established the Army's bureau system and formalized the lines of authority between staff and line; advocated an expansible regular Army in lieu of dependence upon militia; created the position of Commanding General of the Army; established the Artillery School of Practice, the Army's first postgraduate school; authorized and instituted reforms at West Point; was Vice President of the United States under John Quincy Adams and Andrew Jackson; resigned in a dispute with Jackson over states' rights and nullification; served in the U.S. Senate from South Carolina, 1832–1843; became a leading spokesman for slavery and states' rights; served as Secretary of State, 1843–1845; served as South Carolina delegate and presiding officer of a rail and waterway convention at Memphis, Tennessee, 1845; was again a U.S. senator from South Carolina, 1845–1850, died in Washington, D.C., on 31 March 1850.

The Artist

John Wesley Jarvis (1780–1840), portrait and miniature painter, engraver, and sculptor, was born in England. His family came to America about 1785, where he was apprenticed to engraver Edward Savage in Philadelphia. He began painting portraits in his early twenties, established a studio in New York City where Henry Inman and John Quidor studied, and became the foremost portrait painter in New York until he was paralyzed in 1834. Secretary Belknap found his portrait of Calhoun at West Point and gathered it into the secretarial collection. Several of his other portraits served as models for artists who contributed to the Army gallery.

JOHN CALDWELL CALHOUN
Monroe Administration

By John Wesley Jarvis
Oil on canvas, 29½″ x 24½″, date unknown

JAMES BARBOUR was born in Barboursville, Orange County, Virginia, on 10 June 1775; studied under James Waddel, a blind Presbyterian minister, at Gordonsville, but attended no institution of higher learning and remained largely self-taught; married Lucy Johnson in 1792; was admitted to the Virginia bar in 1794 after private study while serving as a deputy sheriff; was elected to the Virginia House of Delegates and served from 1798 to 1804 and from 1808 to 1812; supported the Virginia Resolutions of 1798 concerning the powers of the central government and the rights of the states, holding himself against "absolute consolidated government"; was speaker of the House of Delegates, 1809–1812; drafted the legislation that established the Virginia Literary Fund and laid the foundation for public education in the state; was elected governor of Virginia and served from 1812 to 1815; served in the United States Senate, 1815–1825; was chairman of the Senate Committees on Military Affairs and Foreign Relations; served as Secretary of War, 7 March 1825–23 May 1828; established the Army's Infantry School of Practice; served as minister to Great Britain, 1828–1829; after a contested election, served temporarily in the House of Delegates, 1830–1831, but was forced to give way to his opponent through a decision of the Committee of Privileges and Elections; retired to private life at Barboursville; presided over the 1839 Whig convention that nominated Harrison and Tyler; served as president of the Virginia Agricultural Society; was actively involved in the efforts of the Orange County Humane Society to educate the children of the poor; died in Barboursville, Virginia, on 7 June 1842.

The Artist

Henry Ulke (1821–1910) was born at Frankenstein, Germany. Educated in Berlin, he studied under the court painter, Professor K. W. Wach, joined the revolutionary army, and was wounded, captured, and imprisoned at Spandau before emigrating to the United States in 1849. After working as a designer and illustrator in New York City, he moved to Washington to become a portraitist of statesmen. In addition to the James Barbour portrait, he painted Secretaries Marcy, Holt, Stanton, Rawlins, and McCrary, and interim secretary Reverdy Johnson for the Army portrait gallery.

JAMES BARBOUR
J. Q. Adams Administration

By Henry Ulke
Oil on canvas, 28″ x 22″, 1873

PETER BUELL PORTER was born at Salisbury, Connecticut, on 14 August 1773; graduated from Yale College in 1791; studied law at Judge Tapping Reeve's school at Litchfield, Connecticut; moved to Canandaigua, New York, in 1795; entered into the practice of law; was clerk of Ontario County, 1797–1805; served in the New York legislature, 1801–1802; moved to Black Rock on the Niagara River; was a member of the firm of Porter, Barton & Company which controlled transportation on the Niagara Falls portage; served in the U.S. House of Representatives, 1809–1813; served on a commission on inland navigation established in 1810 to survey a Lake Erie–Hudson River canal route; was a leading figure among Congressional "war hawks" and chairman of the committee that recommended preparation for war with Great Britain; was quartermaster general of New York militia, May–October 1812; participated in and criticized General Alexander Smyth's abortive operations against British Canada, 1812; fought a bloodless duel with Smyth; raised and commanded a brigade of New York militia that incorporated a Six Nations Indian contingent; led his command with distinction in the battles of Chippewa, Lundy's Lane, and Fort Erie, 1814; again served in the Congress, 1814–1816; served on the U.S.–Canadian boundary commission, 1816–1822; was Secretary of State of New York, 1816–1817; was defeated by De Witt Clinton for the New York governorship; married Letitia Breckinridge, 1818; was a regent of the State University, 1824–1830; served as Secretary of War, 26 May 1828–9 March 1829; advocated removal of Eastern Indians beyond the Mississippi; retired to private life; died at Niagara Falls, New York, on 20 March 1844.

The Artist

Daniel Huntington (1816–1906), the New York portrait, historical, and landscape painter, faced the same problems that confronted several of his fellow artists who were commissioned in the 1870's to execute portraits of early Secretaries of War. To produce likenesses that were reasonably contemporary to a subject's stewardship, especially when the office-holder had served before the inception of the daguerreotype and photography and was no longer living to pass upon the finished work, the artist had no recourse except to consult a predecessor's work. Huntington's portrait of Porter falls into this category.

PETER BUELL PORTER
J. Q. Adams Administration

By Daniel Huntington after Matthew Harris Jouett
Oil on canvas, 29½″ x 24½″, 1873

JOHN HENRY EATON was born in Halifax County, North Carolina, on 18 June 1790; attended the University of North Carolina at sixteen; later studied law; moved to Tennessee about 1808 and settled at Franklin in Williamson County where his father had acquired some land; served as a private soldier in the War of 1812; married his first wife, Myra Lewis, a ward of General Andrew Jackson; wrote *The Life of Andrew Jackson, Major General in the Service of the United States,* published in 1817; became a speculator in Florida land; was appointed to the U.S. Senate from Tennessee to fill an unexpired term, 1818; was elected by the state legislature to fill that seat in his own right and served to 1829; married Margaret "Peggy" O'Neale, daughter of a Washington tavern keeper and recent widow of a seaman, January 1829; was selected by President Jackson to be Secretary of War in his new administration despite a clamor raised by several cabinet wives and the local elite who considered the new Mrs. Eaton to be unacceptable to Washington society; served as Secretary of War, 9 March 1829–18 June 1831; advocated compensation upon discharge for soldiers who served honorably; made the Topographical Engineers a separate bureau; resigned the secretaryship as the controversy concerning his wife nourished factionalism that helped rupture the cabinet; was defeated for reelection to the Senate, 1833; served as governor of Florida, 1834–1836; served as minister to Spain, 1836–1840; retired to private life in the nation's capital; died in Washington on 17 November 1856.

The Artist

Robert Walter Weir (1803–1889), longtime professor and instructor in drawing at West Point, painted not only Secretary Eaton but also Secretaries Monroe, Spencer, and Wilkins and interim Secretary Butler for the Army portrait gallery. The portraits were executed in 1873, long after the subjects had died, forcing Weir and his associates in the Army project to make good use of available graphic documentation.

JOHN HENRY EATON
Jackson Administration

By Robert Walter Weir
Oil on canvas, 29½″ x 24½″, 1873

LEWIS CASS was born in Exeter, New Hampshire, on 9 October 1782; attended Exeter Academy; taught school in Wilmington, Delaware, 1799; moved to Marietta, Ohio, 1800, where he entered the practice of law in 1802; moved to Zanesville, Ohio; married Elizabeth Spencer, 1806; was elected to the Ohio legislature, 1806; served as marshal of Ohio, 1807–1812; was appointed colonel of the 3d Ohio Regiment and served with Generals Hull and Harrison in operations in the Old Northwest in the War of 1812; was commissioned a colonel and then brigadier general in the Regular Army, 1813; held joint command with Harrison of the Eighth Military District; participated in the Battle of the Thames, 1813; served as governor of Michigan Territory, 1813–1831; served concurrently as superintendent of Indian affairs of the region, negotiating treaties with several tribes; served as Secretary of War, 1 August 1831–5 October 1836; superintended the removal of Eastern Indians to trans-Mississippi lands; recommended a public armory for fabrication of cannon; recommended establishment of a regiment of dragoons; pressed for a plan for the efficient organization of the militia; was appointed minister to France, 1836; served in the U.S. Senate from Michigan, 1845–1848; was nominated for President on the Democratic ticket, 1848; again served in the U.S. Senate, 1849–1857; served as Secretary of State, 1857–1860, and resigned in protest over the government's decision not to reinforce Fort Sumter and the Charleston defenses; returned to his home in Detroit and continued to write in retirement on Indian and Western subjects; died there on 17 June 1866.

The Artist

Daniel Huntington (1816–1906) was a student at Hamilton College in Utica, New York, while Lewis Cass was Secretary of War. He had advanced in his profession to become president of the prestigious National Academy of Design by the time Cass died in 1866 and painted the former secretary's portrait seven years later. Huntington produced some 1,200 works during his artistic career, about 1,000 of them portraits. Fifteen of his portraits were of primary (nominated and confirmed) Secretaries of War.

LEWIS CASS
Jackson Administration

By Daniel Huntington
Oil on canvas, 29½″ x 24½″, 1873

JOEL ROBERTS POINSETT was born in Charleston, South Carolina, on 2 March 1779; was educated by his father and the Reverend J. H. Thompson of Charleston; attended the academy of Timothy Dwight at Greenfield Hill, Connecticut, 1794; continued his studies abroad; visited Portugal for reasons of health; returned home to study law under H. W. De Saussure; toured Europe and Asia in 1801–1804 and 1806–1808; returned home amid indications of war with Great Britain; was a special agent to the South American states, 1810–1814; returned to South Carolina in 1815; served in the state legislature, 1816–1820; was chairman of the state's Board of Public Works, 1818–1820; served in the U.S. House of Representatives, 1821–1825; served as a special envoy to Mexico, 1822-1823; was appointed the first American minister to Mexico, 1825, and became embroiled in the country's political turmoil until his recall in 1830; returned to South Carolina to espouse the Unionist cause in nullification quarrels, 1830–1833; married Mary Izard Pringle, 1833; served as Secretary of War, 7 March 1837–5 March 1841; presided over the continuing removal of Indians west of the Mississippi and over the Seminole War; reduced the fragmentation of the Army by concentrating elements at central locations; equipped the light batteries of artillery regiments as authorized by the 1821 army organization act; again retired to his plantation at Georgetown, South Carolina, 1841; developed the poinsettia from a Mexican flower; was a founder of the National Institute for the Promotion of Science and the Useful Arts, 1840; died near Statesburg, South Carolina, on 12 December 1851.

The Artist

Army records note that Secretary Poinsett's portrait was painted by an unknown artist at an unknown place and date and was already in the department's possession when the portrait gallery project was launched in 1873, but records also indicate that Robert Walter Weir painted Poinsett for the collection. Although the Poinsett work seems to fall within the Weir style as seen in his portraits of Secretaries Monroe, Eaton, Spencer, and Wilkins, the lack of signature, date and substantive documentary record leaves the matter in doubt.

JOEL ROBERTS POINSETT
Van Buren Administration

By an unknown artist
Oil on canvas, 29½″ x 24½″, date unknown

JOHN BELL was born on his father's farm near Nashville, Tennessee, on 15 February 1797; graduated from Cumberland College in 1814 at seventeen; was admitted to the bar and began practice in Franklin, Tennessee; was elected to the state legislature before reaching twenty-one; moved to Nashville to continue the practice of law, circa 1819; married Sally Dickinson and, following her death, Jane Yeatman; served in the U.S. House of Representatives from Tennessee, 1827–1841; served as Speaker of the House, 1834–1835, defeating James K. Polk who was also a candidate for the office; although originally a member of President Jackson's party and a supporter of administration policies, opposed Jackson's bank policy and selection of Van Buren as a successor; became the leader of the Whig party in Tennessee; served as Secretary of War in the Harrison and Tyler cabinets, 5 March 1841–13 September 1841; presided over the final stages of the Seminole War; returned to private life, 1841–1847; was elected to the U.S. Senate in 1847 and served to 1859; remained a nationally–minded Southerner in the Congress as sectional attitudes sharpened over the slavery issue; was the presidential candidate of the Constitutional Union Party in 1860; at first opposed secession and influenced Tennessee's decision not to secede; after Fort Sumter, supported his state's decision to join the Confederacy; moved to the lower South after Union troops entered Tennessee; returned home after the Civil War; died near Bear Spring Furnace, Stewart County, Tennessee, on 10 September 1869.

The Artist

Thomas Le Clear (1818–1882), portrait and genre painter, showed artistic aptitude in childhood: he sold his first work when he was twelve and engaged in portrait and decorative painting while yet in his teens. He was born at Owego, New York, and lived with his family in various locations in New York, Ontario, and Wisconsin before settling in New York City in 1839. From 1844 to 1860, he lived in Buffalo, then returned to New York City to continue his art career. Elected a National Academician in 1863, his work is represented in the collections of the Maryland Historical Society in Baltimore and the Corcoran Gallery of Art in Washington, D.C.

JOHN BELL
W. H. Harrison and Tyler Administrations

By Thomas Le Clear
Oil on canvas (tondo), 29″ x 24″, 1874

JOHN CANFIELD SPENCER was born in Hudson, New York, on 8 January 1788; entered college at Williamstown, Massachusetts, transferred to Union College, Schenectady, New York, and graduated with honors in 1806; became secretary to Governor Daniel D. Tompkins, 1807; studied law in Albany and was admitted to the bar, 1809; married Elizabeth Scott Smith, 1809; moved to Canandaigua, New York; entered the practice of law there and became a master of chancery, 1811; was appointed brigade judge advocate on the northern frontier, 1813; was postmaster at Canandaigua, 1814; became assistant attorney general and district attorney for the five western counties of New York, 1815; served in the U.S. House of Representatives, 1817–1819; was a member of the committee that reported unfavorably on the affairs of the National Bank; was nominated but defeated for the U.S. Senate; served in the state assembly, 1820–1822; served in the state senate, 1825–1828; became special prosecutor to investigate the disappearance of William Morgan, author of a manuscript on Masonic rituals, 1829; again served in the state legislature, 1831–1833; moved to Albany, 1837; edited an English edition of De Tocqueville's *Democracy in America,* 1838; was secretary of state of New York, 1839; served as Secretary of War, 12 October 1841–3 March 1843; proposed a chain of posts extending from Council Bluffs, Iowa, to the Columbia River; urged that the government adhere to field commander arrangements by compensating the Creek Indians who were removed; lost his son Philip, who was executed for attempted mutiny aboard the brig *Somers,* 1842; was nominated to the Supreme Court but rejected by the U.S. Senate, 1844; died in Albany, New York, on 18 May 1855.

The Artist

Robert Walter Weir (1803–1889), landscape, portrait, and genre painter, illustrator, and a National Academician, was instructor in drawing at the United States Military Academy when Secretary Spencer presided over the War Department. Although Spencer may well have visited West Point in the discharge of his official duties, Weir did not have the opportunity to paint him from life. The portrait was not painted until three decades later, eighteen years after Spencer's death.

JOHN CANFIELD SPENCER
Tyler Administration

By Robert Walter Weir
Oil on canvas, 29½″ x 24½″, 1873

JAMES MADISON PORTER was born near Norristown, Pennsylvania, on 6 January 1793; received his early education in the home, then attended Norristown Academy; began the study of law in an office at Lancaster, Pennsylvania, 1809; joined his brother, Judge Robert Porter, to study law at Reading; moved to Philadelphia to clerk in the prothonotary's office, 1812; helped raise and officer a volunteer militia company to garrison Fort Mifflin, 1813; advanced to the rank of colonel; was admitted to the bar and began the practice of law, 1813; moved to Easton, 1818; was appointed deputy attorney general for Northhampton County; married Eliza Michler, 1821; was instrumental in the founding of Lafayette College, 1826; was president of its board of trustees, 1826–1852, and professor of jurisprudence and political economy, 1837–1852; was appointed to a vacancy as president judge of the Twelfth Judicial District, 1839; resigned in 1840 and returned to the practice of law; was nominated by President Tyler to be Secretary of War, 1843, and served 8 March 1843–30 January 1844; directed the preparation of a history of the Indian tribes; was ultimately rejected by the Senate, 30 January 1844; was elected to the state legislature, 1849; served as chairman of the judiciary committee; served as president judge of the Twenty-second Judicial District, 1853–1855; was president of the Delaware, Lehigh, Schuylkill & Susquehanna Railroad, 1847–1853, continuing when it became the Lehigh Valley Railroad, 1853–1856; became president of the Belvidere Delaware Railroad; died at Easton, Pennsylvania, on 11 November 1862.

The Artist

Daniel Huntington (1816–1906), New York portrait, landscape, and historical painter, National Academician, and twice president of the National Academy of Design (1862–1870 and 1877–1890), drew upon the work of a provincial artist to execute his portrait of Secretary James M. Porter. He painted it three decades after the subject held office and a dozen years after his death. Huntington was a key artist in the creation of the Army portrait gallery; his contribution is of major significance as to both quantity and quality.

JAMES MADISON PORTER
Tyler Administration

By Daniel Huntington
Oil on canvas, 29″ x 24″, 1874

WILLIAM WILKINS was born in Carlisle, Pennsylvania, on 20 December 1779; moved with his family to Pittsburgh in 1783; graduated from Dickinson College, Carlisle, in 1802; studied law with David Watts at Carlisle; returned to Pittsburgh and was admitted to the Allegheny County bar; was censured in 1806 for participating as a second in a duel; was an organizer of the Pittsburgh Manufacturing Company; became its president when it was chartered in 1814 as the Bank of Pittsburgh; was president of the Monongahela Bridge Company; was president of the Greensburg and Pittsburgh Turnpike Company; married Catherine Holmes, 1815, who died the following year; was president of the Pittsburgh Common Council, 1816–1819; married Mathilda Dallas, 1818; was elected to the state legislature, 1819; resigned in December 1820 to become presiding judge of the Fifth Judicial District; was appointed judge of the U.S. District Court for Western Pennsylvania, 1824; was an unsuccessful candidate for the U.S. House of Representatives, 1826; was elected to the House in 1828 but resigned before taking office; was elected to the U.S. Senate in 1831; resigned to accept appointment as minister to Russia, 1834–1836; was again defeated as a candidate for Congress, 1840; was again elected to the U.S. House of Representatives, 1842–1843; served as Secretary of War, 15 February 1844–4 March 1845; espoused territorial expansion and favored the annexation of Texas; returned to private life in Pittsburgh; served in the Pennsylvania Senate, 1855–1857; became major general in the Pennsylvania Home Guard, 1862; lived in retirement in Pittsburgh; died there on 23 June 1865.

The Artist

Rober Walter Weir (1803–1889) is second only to Daniel Huntington in the number of portraits he produced for the Army portrait gallery. Weir received $300 each for his portraits of Secretaries Monroe, Eaton, Spencer, Wilkins, and interim Secretary Butler. When Secretary Belknap's portrait project, begun in the centennial year, was terminated in the bicentennial year, the taxpayer's investment appeared to have been well secured. The five Weir paintings, produced in the 1870's at a total cost of $1,500, were appraised in the 1970's at slightly more than $10,000.

WILLIAM WILKINS
Tyler Administration

By Robert Walter Weir
Oil on canvas, 29½″ x 24½″, 1873

WILLIAM LEARNED MARCY was born in Sturbridge (now Southbridge), Massachusetts, on 12 December 1786; was educated at Leicester and Woodstock Academies; graduated from Brown University, 1808; taught school briefly at Newport, Rhode Island; moved to Troy, New York, to study law and was admitted to the bar, 1811; married Dolly Newell in 1812 (deceased in 1821); wrote for the *Northern Budget* and the *Albany Argus*; joined the 155th New York Regiment and served in several actions of the War of 1812; was appointed adjutant general of New York, 1821; was appointed recorder of Troy, 1816–1818 and 1821–1823; was an associate in the firm of Marcy & Lane, 1818–1823; was appointed state comptroller of New York and moved to Albany, 1823; married Cornelia Knower, circa 1825; was appointed associate justice of the state Supreme Court, 1829; was elected to the U.S. Senate, 1831–1832; served three terms as governor of New York, 1833–1838; executed the state's first survey of fifty-six counties; was a member of the Mexican Claims Commission, 1840–1842; served as Secretary of War, 6 March 1845–4 March 1849; recommended augmentation of existing Army units to meet a growing threat from Mexico and the Indians; proposed establishment of an Indian agency in the Oregon territory to deal with northwestern tribes; was a key figure in the settlement of the Oregon boundary dispute, 1846; served as Secretary of State, 7 March 1853–6 March 1857, and directed the negotiation of twenty-four pacts, including the Gadsden Treaty which added 29,640 square miles to the U.S.; returned to private life in Albany; died at Ballston Spa, New York, on 4 July 1857.

The Artist

Henry Ulke (1821–1910), a German-born and German-trained artist and a court painter and revolutionary in Berlin before he emigrated to the United States in 1849, was next only to Huntington and Weir in the number of portraits he contributed to the first century of the War Department's secretarial gallery project. His portraits of six of Secretary Belknap's predecessors—Barbour, Marcy, Holt, Stanton, Rawlins, Johnson—and one successor—McCrary—were among the more than one hundred he produced while a limner of statesmen in the nation's capital.

WILLIAM LEARNED MARCY
Polk Administration

By Henry Ulke
Oil on canvas, 27¾″ x 22¼″, 1873

GEORGE WASHINGTON CRAWFORD was born in Columbia County near Augusta, Georgia, on 22 December 1798; graduated from Princeton College in 1820; studied law and was admitted to the bar in 1822; entered the practice of law, opening an office in Augusta; was elected attorney general of Georgia and served in the period 1827–1831; returned to the practice of law; served in the Georgia legislature from 1837 to 1842; was elected to the U.S. House of Representatives as a Whig in 1843 and served about one month, resigning to accept the nomination for governor; served as governor of Georgia for two terms, 1843–1847; served as Secretary of War in President Taylor's cabinet, 8 March 1849–23 July 1850; proposed that a bounty be granted to encourage enlistees to enter service at remote stations; resigned upon President Taylor's death; retired to private life at his Georgia home; served as chairman of the Georgia secession convention, 1861; died at his Bel Air estate near Augusta on 22 July 1872. (Secretary Crawford's middle name is given as Walker in some sources.)

The Artist

Daniel Huntington (1816–1906), well-known New York painter and the major contributor to the War Department secretarial portrait gallery, received $300 for his portrait of Secretary Belknap and for each portrait of eight of Belknap's predecessors, including Secretary Crawford. As fine art tends to increase in value with time, these nine Huntington portraits, commissioned for the nation's 1876 centennial celebration at a total cost to the department of $2,700, were appraised in the 1976 bicentennial year at $15,300. Huntington's portrait of Secretary Crawford is after one by Alexander Hay Ritchie (1822–1895).

GEORGE WASHINGTON CRAWFORD
Taylor Administration

By Daniel Huntington after Alexander Hay Ritchie
Oil on canvas, 29½″ x 24½″, 1873

CHARLES MAGILL CONRAD was born in Winchester, Frederick County, Virginia, on 24 December 1804; moved to Mississippi with his family as a boy; moved to Louisiana and was educated under a Dr. Huld at New Orleans; studied law in the office of Abner L. Duncan in that city; fought a duel in which he killed his opponent; was admitted to the bar and began the practice of law in New Orleans, 1828; married M. W. Angella Lewis; was elected to the Louisiana legislature in 1840 and served two terms; was appointed to the U.S. Senate in April 1842 to fill the unexpired term of Alexander Mouton, serving to March 1843; was defeated for reelection in his own right; served as a delegate to the Louisiana state constitutional convention, 1844; served in the U.S. House of Representatives, 1849–1850; resigned to accept appointment as Secretary of War in President Fillmore's cabinet; served as Secretary of War, 15 August 1850–7 March 1853; recommended that another mounted regiment be raised for Indian service; proposed that local militia, provided with government arms, be formed to meet the Indian threat; urged that the government feed Indians who would abandon predatory habits and cultivate the soil; resumed the practice of law; served as a delegate from New Orleans to the state convention to ratify national and state tickets, 1860; served as a delegate to the Provisional Confederate Congress, February 1861; served as a representative from Louisiana to the Confederate Congress, 1862–1864; lost his estate through confiscation; resumed the practice of law after the Civil War; suffered a seizure while testifying in federal circuit court in New Orleans, 1878; died in New Orleans on 11 February 1878.

The Artist

Daniel Huntington (1816–1906) painted presidents and generals, writers and artists, Astors and Vanderbilts in seven active decades as a working artist. Despite the fact that he achieved prominence in his day, he has been largely ignored by art historians, suggesting that what Richard Muther wrote of the French artist Leon Cogniet (1794–1880) applies in some degree to Huntington: "As an artist he belongs to the list of great men who have paid for overpraise in their lifetime by oblivion after their death." Huntington painted Charles M. Conrad twenty years after his subject's Army stewardship and five years before Conrad's death.

CHARLES MAGILL CONRAD
Fillmore Administration

By Daniel Huntington
Oil on canvas, 29½″ x 24½″, 1873

JEFFERSON DAVIS was born in Christian (now Todd) County, Kentucky, on 3 June 1808; moved with his family to Wilkinson County, Mississippi; attended St. Thomas's Seminary, 1815, and Transylvania University, 1821; graduated from West Point, 1828; was assigned to frontier service in Wisconsin-Illinois; participated in the Black Hawk War, 1832; resigned his commission, 1835; married and lost his first wife Sarah Knox Taylor, daughter of Zachary Taylor, 1835; was a planter in Mississippi, 1835–1845; married Varina Howell, 1845; served in the U.S. House of Representatives, 1845–1846; resigned to take part in the Mexican War and participated in the battles of Monterey and Buena Vista, 1846–1847; served in the U.S. Senate, 1847–1851; was an unsuccessful candidate for governor of Mississippi, 1851; served as Secretary of War, 7 March 1853–6 March 1857; sponsored Army map and route surveys of the trans-Mississippi West, experimented with a camel corps, obtained four new regiments for the Army, and sponsored the adoption of a new rifled infantry musket; was again elected to the U.S. Senate, 1857–1861; announced the secession of Mississippi and tendered his resignation, 21 January 1861; was appointed major general of Mississippi militia; was appointed President of the Confederate States of America by a provisional Congress, 18 February 1861, elected by popular vote, and inaugurated as President, 22 February 1862; fled Richmond as Union troops advanced, 3 April 1865; was captured at Irwinville, Georgia, and interned at Fortress Monroe, Virginia; refused to ask for Federal pardon; was released on bond, 13 May 1867; retired to Mississippi; died in New Orleans on 6 December 1889; full rights of citizenship restored by the U.S. Congress, 1978.

The Artist

Daniel Huntington (1816–1906) was at the midpoint of his career when he painted Secretary Davis in 1874; he had first exhibited circa 1836 at the National Academy of Design in New York when he was only twenty, and would paint until the year of his death, 1906. Jefferson Davis's tour in the department was seventeen years in the past when Huntington painted him, and, although Davis was still living, Huntington's portrait of him was after a copy rather than from life.

JEFFERSON DAVIS
Pierce Administration

By Daniel Huntington
Oil on canvas, 29½″ x 24½″, 1874

JOHN BUCHANAN FLOYD was born in Smithfield, Virginia, on 1 June 1806; was educated by gifted parents; was probably a student at Georgetown College, Washington, D.C., before transferring to South Carolina College, from which he graduated in 1829; married Sally Preston in 1830; entered the practice of law at Wytheville, Virginia; moved to Arkansas to take up cotton planting and practice law at Helena; was stricken along with many of his slaves by malignant fever; returned to Virginia to recuperate and resume his law practice, 1837; was elected to the state legislature in 1847 and 1848; was governor of Virginia, 1849–1852; resumed the practice of law at Abingdon, Virginia; was again elected to the General Assembly, 1855; served as Secretary of War, 6 March 1857–29 December 1860; disagreed with the government's decision to sustain Major Anderson's occupation of Fort Sumter; was asked to resign for accepting drafts by government contractors against future services; departed office amid complaints he had transferred arms to Southern arsenals in anticipation of approaching war; was investigated by a congressional committee but no action resulted, 1861; was appointed brigadier general in the Confederate Army; participated in actions with Lee's Army in West Virginia; was removed from command by Jefferson Davis for his conduct at Fort Donelson, Tennessee, 1862; was promoted to major general by the Virginia legislature; died at Abingdon, Virginia, on 26 August 1863; was later held (1868) by a divided Supreme Court to have been in violation of the law for the contractor acceptances honored in advance during his administration of the War Department.

The Artist

Daniel Huntington (1816–1906) was not only a National Academician and twice president of the National Academy of Design, but also a founder of the Century Club and its president for sixteen years, and a vice president and trustee of the Metropolitan Museum of Art in New York. A self-portrait hangs in the Century Club, and his work is represented in public and private collections around the country, including the White House (President and Mrs. Rutherford B. Hayes, President Chester A. Arthur, Mrs. Benjamin Harrison) and the Capitol (Speaker Robert C. Winthrop). His portrait of Secretary Floyd was executed more than a decade after the subject's death.

JOHN BUCHANAN FLOYD
Buchanan Administration

By Daniel Huntington
Oil on canvas, 29½″ x 24½″, 1874

JOSEPH HOLT was born in Breckenridge County, Kentucky, on 6 January 1807; was educated at St. Joseph's College, Bardstown, and Centre College, Danville; entered into the practice of law at Elizabethtown, Kentucky, 1828; married Mary Harrison; moved to Louisville, 1832; was assistant editor of the *Louisville Advertiser*; was commonwealth's attorney, 1833-1835; moved to Port Gibson, Mississippi, to practice law, 1835–1842; returned to Louisville to recuperate from tuberculosis after losing his wife to the disease; continued to practice law; married Margaret Wickliffe; moved to Washington to serve as commissioner of patents, 1857–1859; served as U.S. postmaster general, 1859–1861; served as Secretary of War, 18 January–5 March 1861; was appointed the first Judge Advocate General of the U.S. Army, 3 September 1862; prosecuted the John Wilkes Booth conspirators in the Lincoln assassination and was accused of suppressing evidence; issued a pamphlet, *Vindication of Judge Advocate General Holt From the Foul Slanders of Traitors, Confessed Perjurers and Suborners, Acting in the Interest of Jefferson Davis,* 1866; resigned as Judge Advocate General, 1875; died in Washington, D.C., on 1 August 1894.

The Artist

Louis P. Spinner, a Washington artist, painted and taught in the nation's capital during the period 1880–1914. Although substantiating records have not been found, his portrait of Secretary Holt may have been commissioned to replace one done from life by Henry Ulke (1821–1910) in 1873 for the secretarial gallery and lost at a later date. Spinner's portrait was done about five years before Secretary Holt's death and appears to be a composite of tinted photography and painting. Although Spinner is thought to have died sometime after 1924, detailed information about him has not come to light.

JOSEPH HOLT
Buchanan Administration

By Louis P. Spinner
Oil on canvas, 28" x 22", 1889

SIMON CAMERON was born in Maytown, Lancaster County, Pennsylvania, on 8 March 1799; was orphaned at nine and later apprenticed to a printer before entering the field of journalism; was editor of the Bucks County *Messenger*, 1821; moved to Washington in 1822 and studied political movements while working for the printing firm of Gales and Seaton; married Margaret Brua; returned to Harrisburg to purchase and run the *Republican*, 1824; served as state printer of Pennsylvania, circa 1825–1827; was state adjutant general, 1826; constructed several rail lines and merged them into the Northern Central Railroad; founded the Bank of Middletown, 1832, and engaged in other business enterprises; was appointed a commissioner to settle claims of the Winnebago Indians, 1838; served in the U.S. Senate, 1845–1849; was again elected to the Senate, 1857–1861; was an unsuccessful candidate for the Republican nomination for president, 1860; served as Secretary of War, 5 March 1861–14 January 1862; centralized recruiting in the War Department; was widely criticized for favoritism in awarding departmental positions and contracts, and was censured by the House of Representatives for contract manipulations; was again elected to the Senate and served from 1867 to 1877; saw his son, James Donald Cameron, appointed Secretary of War, 1876; resigned his Senate seat upon assurances from the subservient Pennsylvania legislature that his son would be elected his successor, 1877; retired to his farm at Donegal Springs, Pennsylvania; died there on 26 June 1889.

The Artist

Freeman Thorp (1844–1922) was born in Geneva, Ohio. He studied portrait painting and at twenty-seven began to paint statesmen in a studio built for his use on the roof of the U.S. Capitol. It was there that Ulysses Grant sat for his portrait. Thorp painted four other presidents—Lincoln, Garfield, McKinley, and Cleveland—among a number of eminent Americans, including Chief Justice Salmon Chase, Horace Greeley, and Robert E. Lee. He was thirty years old when he painted Secretary Cameron, who, although a dozen years beyond his War Department stewardship, was still sitting in the Senate.

SIMON CAMERON
Lincoln Administration

By Freeman Thorp
Oil on canvas, 29¼" x 24¼", 1874

EDWIN McMASTERS STANTON was born in Steubenville, Ohio, on 19 December 1814; left school as a teenager, upon his father's death, to work and continued spare time study, 1827; attended Kenyon College but withdrew for financial reasons; studied law and was admitted to the bar, 1836; married Mary Ann Lamson; was prosecuting attorney of Harrison County, Ohio, 1837–1839; entered the practice of law at Cadiz and Steubenville, 1839; lost his wife, 1844; moved to Pittsburgh to pursue his law career, 1847; was counsel for the state of Pennsylvania, 1849–1856; married Ellen Hutchinson, 1856; was appointed a special government counsel to adjudicate fraudulent land claims in California, 1858; was attorney general of the United States, 1860–1861; served as Secretary of War, 20 January 1862–28 May 1868; persuaded Congress that the government should assume selective control over the railroads and telegraph; prevailed upon the president to release political prisoners in military custody and transfer control over extraordinary arrests from the State to the War Department; established a Bureau of Colored Troops; rejected President Andrew Johnson's August 1867 request that he resign; was suspended by President Johnson but resumed his seat when the Senate nonconcurred, January 1868; resigned in May 1868; resumed the practice of law; was nominated by President Grant to be an associate justice of the Supreme Court and was confirmed by the Senate on 20 December 1869, but died in Washington, D.C., on 24 December 1869 before he could take office.

The Artist

Henry Ulke (1821–1910), German-born and German-trained, was active as an illustrator and designer from his arrival in New York City in 1849 until his move to Washington in 1857. Switching from illustration to fine art, he painted over a hundred portraits, mostly of eminent Americans, in his more than half a century of activity in the nation's capital. In addition to half a dozen Secretaries of War, he painted a number of Secretaries of the Treasury and such notable figures as Chief Justices Salmon Chase and Roger Taney, Secretary of State James G. Blaine, Senator Charles Sumner, and Mrs. Jefferson Davis.

EDWIN McMASTERS STANTON
Lincoln and A. Johnson Administrations

By Henry Ulke
Oil on canvas, 28″ x 22″, 1872

JOHN McALLISTER SCHOFIELD was born in Gerry, New York, on 29 December 1831; moved to Freeport, Illinois, 1843; graduated from West Point, 1853; served with 2d Artillery in Georgia and the 1st Artillery in Florida, 1853–1855; taught natural and experimental philosophy at West Point, 1855–1857; married his first wife, Harriet Bartlett, 1857; taught physics at Washington University, St. Louis, 1860; was detailed at the outbreak of the Civil War as mustering officer in Missouri; was major of the 1st Missouri Volunteer Infantry; moved up to command the Army of the Frontier in Missouri operations, 1862–1863; commanded the Department of the Missouri, 1863; commanded the XXIII Corps, 1864; participated in the battles of Franklin and Nashville; was commissioned brigadier general in the regular Army, 1864; commanded the Department of North Carolina; participated with Sherman's forces in final operations in the South; was dispatched to France as confidential agent to deal with Mexican affairs, 1865–1866; commanded the Department of the Potomac, 1867; served as Secretary of War, 1 June 1868–13 March 1869; recommended that the management of Indian affairs be restored to the War Department; was promoted to major general and command of the Department of the Missouri; commanded the Division of the Pacific; served as superintendent of the U.S. Military Academy, 1876–1881; successively commanded the divisions of the Pacific, Missouri, and Atlantic; served as commanding general of the Army, 1888–1895; married Georgia Kilbourne, 1891; was promoted to lieutenant general and retired, 1895; died in St. Augustine, Florida, on 4 March 1906.

The Artist

Stephen William Shaw (1817–1900) was born in Windsor, Vermont. At thirty-one he journeyed to California by way of New Orleans and Panama to settle at San Francisco and pursue a career as a portrait painter. He became the official artist to the Masonic order there, painting a large number of Masons and other Western notables. He also participated in the expedition that discovered Humboldt Bay in New Guinea. Shaw painted Secretary Schofield from life in 1874 while his subject was commander of the Military Division of the Pacific with headquarters at San Francisco.

JOHN McALLISTER SCHOFIELD
A. Johnson Administration

By Stephen William Shaw
Oil on canvas, 30″ x 25″, 1874

JOHN AARON RAWLINS was born in Galena, Illinois, on 13 February 1831; attended local schools followed by eighteen months at Rock River Seminary at Mount Morris, Illinois; studied law in the office of Isaac P. Stevens of Galena and was admitted to the bar in 1854; practiced law in partnership with Stevens and later with one of his own pupils, David Sheean; married his first wife, Emily Smith, 1856; was city attorney in 1857; was nominated a presidential elector on the Douglas ticket, 1860; helped organize the 45th Illinois Infantry and was designated a major in the regiment; was requested by Colonel Ulysses S. Grant of the 21st Illinois Infantry to accept a commission as lieutenant and assignment as Grant's aide-de-camp; was appointed captain and assistant adjutant general of volunteers on Grant's staff, 1861; lost his wife to tuberculosis; served as Grant's principal adviser; was promoted to major in May 1862, lieutenant colonel in November 1862, and brigadier general of volunteers, August 1863; married Mary Hurlbut, 1863; was designated chief of staff of the Army, 1865; was brevetted major general of volunteers in February 1865 and of the regular army in April 1865; contracted tuberculosis; attempted to restore his health by accompanying Grenville Dodge on a survey of the proposed route of the Union Pacific Railroad to Salt Lake City; served as Secretary of War, 13 March 1869–6 September 1869; died in office in Washington, D.C., on 6 September 1869.

The Artist

Henry Ulke (1821–1910), the German-born artist who left revolutionary activities behind when he emigrated to the United States in 1849, became not only a leading portrait painter in his adopted land but also a celebrated naturalist as well; his collection of American beetles, the largest known at the time, was exhibited in the Museum of Natural History at the Carnegie Institute in Pittsburgh. Ulke would undoubtedly have painted Secretary Rawlins from life had the Army official not succumbed to tuberculosis. Rawlins had been dead about four years when Ulke produced his portrait for the Army gallery.

JOHN AARON RAWLINS
Grant Administration

By Henry Ulke
Oil on canvas, 28″ x 22½″, 1873

WILLIAM WORTH BELKNAP was born in Newburgh, New York, on 22 September 1829; graduated from Princeton University in 1848; studied law at Georgetown University, Washington, D.C.; was admitted to the bar, 1851; moved to Keokuk, Iowa, and entered the practice of law; served in the state legislature, 1857–1858; was commissioned major in the 15th Iowa Infantry, 1861; participated in the Civil War battles of Shiloh, Corinth, and Vicksburg; was promoted to brigadier general and given command of the 4th Division, XVII Corps, 1864; participated in General Sherman's operations in Georgia and the Carolinas; was mustered out of service as a major general, 1865; married and lost his first two wives, Cora LeRoy and Carrie Tomlinson, and married Mrs. John Bower, his second wife's sister; was collector of internal revenue in Iowa, 1865–1869; served as Secretary of War, 25 October 1869–2 March 1876; launched the secretarial portrait gallery, circa 1872; recommended that Congress act to fix May 1 as the start of the fiscal year; inaugurated the preparation of historical reports by post commanders; proposed actions to preserve Yellowstone Park; was impeached by a unanimous vote of the House of Representatives for allegedly having received money in return for post tradership appointments; resigned the secretaryship before being brought to trial, March 1876; was tried by the United States Senate, but the vote fell short of the two-thirds required for conviction; moved to Philadelphia, then returned to Washington to resume the practice of law; died in Washington, D.C., on 13 October 1890.

The Artist

Daniel Huntington (1816–1906), who produced a larger number of secretarial portraits than any other artist, and Secretary Belknap, who created the portrait gallery, came together in a direct association in 1874 when Huntington painted the sitting secretary from life. With the line of descent brought up to date, a new era opened. Secretaries began to select their own portraitists, and the artists began to paint their subjects from life. The first century with its predominance of copy work gave way to a second century marked by an interplay of personal relationships that is reflected in the official portraiture.

WILLIAM WORTH BELKNAP
Grant Administration

By Daniel Huntington
Oil on canvas, 29½″ x 24½″, 1874

ALPHONSO TAFT was born in Townshend, Vermont, on 5 November 1810; attended local schools and taught school to obtain funds to study at Amherst Academy; graduated from Yale College, 1833; taught school at Ellington, Connecticut; held a tutorship at Yale while studying law; was admitted to the Connecticut bar, 1838; moved to Cincinnati and commenced the practice of law, circa 1840; married Fanny Phelps, 1841, and, after her death, Louisa Torrey, 1853; was appointed to the superior court of Cincinnati to fill a vacancy, then elected to the post for two terms, 1865–1872; resumed the practice of law, 1872–1876; served as Secretary of War, 8 March–22 May 1876; was appointed attorney general of the United States, 1876–1877; was an unsuccessful candidate for governor of Ohio, 1875 and 1879; served as minister to Austria-Hungary, 1882–1884; served as minister to Russia, 1885–1886; died in San Diego, California, on 21 May 1891.

The Artist

Daniel Huntington (1816–1906) had completed four of his seven decades as a working artist and had secured his reputation as a portrait, historical, and landscape painter when Secretary Alphonso Taft sat for him during the nation's centennial year. The Army increased the fee for secretarial portraits from $300 to $500, effective with Huntington's work on Taft, an increase fully justified in light of the additional requirements of painting from life — requirements involving appointments, sittings, and approvals.

ALPHONSO TAFT
Grant Administration

By Daniel Huntington
Oil on canvas, 29½″ x 24½″, 1876

JAMES DONALD CAMERON was born in Middletown, Pennsylvania, on 14 May 1833; graduated from Princeton University in 1852; clerked in the Bank of Middletown founded by his father, Simon Cameron; moved up to cashier and finally president of the bank; married Mary McCormick, who died in 1874; during the Civil War supervised the transportation of Union troops over the Northern Central Railroad, one of his father's enterprises; was president of the railroad from 1863 to 1874; was active in coal, iron, and manufacturing interests; joined with his father in dominating Pennsylvania politics; was a delegate to the Republican national conventions of 1868 and 1880; served as Secretary of War, 22 May 1876–3 March 1877; requested legislation requiring contractors to stand on their bids for specified periods of time; requested authorization to devote a portion of the funds allocated to publishing War of the Rebellion records to the preservation of the Matthew Brady photo collection; was elected to fill the unexpired term of his father in the U.S. Senate after his father resigned to make way for him, 1877–1879; was returned to the Senate for three terms, serving from 1879 to 1897; married General Sherman's niece, Elizabeth Sherman, 1878; was chairman of the Republican national committee, 1879; retired from public life to live on his Lancaster farm and devote his time to private affairs; died on 30 August 1918.

The Artist

Daniel Huntington (1816–1906) made his mark upon the Army's portrait collection not only in the number of paintings he executed but also in the variety and distinction of his subjects. In addition to his contribution to the secretarial line of succession, he painted two distinguished Revolutionary War soldiers, George Washington and Horatio Gates; one notable Mexican War commander, Winfield Scott; and three eminent Civil War leaders, Ulysses S. Grant, William T. Sherman, and Philip H. Sheridan. All but Washington had direct official connections to the administration of the War Department. Huntington's portrait of Secretary Cameron was painted from life.

JAMES DONALD CAMERON
Grant Administration

By Daniel Huntington
Oil on canvas, 29½″ x 24½″, 1877

GEORGE WASHINGTON McCRARY was born near Evansville, Indiana, on 29 August 1835; moved with his family to Van Buren County, Iowa, 1837; was educated at regional schools and taught in a country school at eighteen; studied law in Keokuk, Iowa, in the office of John W. Rankin and Samuel F. Miller; was admitted to the bar in 1856; married Helen Gelatt, 1857; served in the state assembly, 1857–1860; served as a state senator, 1861–1865; was elected to the U.S. House of Representatives and served from 1869 to 1877; was chairman of the committee on elections; published *A Treatise on the American Law of Elections*, 1875; helped create the Electoral Commission; served on the committee that investigated the Credit Mobilier scandal; was a member of the Committee on the Judiciary and the Committee on Canals and Railroads; served as Secretary of War, 12 March 1877–10 December 1879; withdrew federal troops from the remaining reconstruction governments in South Carolina and Louisiana; used federal troops in the 1877 railway strike and in Mexican border disturbances; became judge of the Eighth Judicial District and served from 1880 to 1884; moved to Kansas City, Missouri, and became general counsel for the Atchison, Topeka & Santa Fe Railroad for the remainder of his active career; died in St. Joseph, Missouri, on 23 June 1890.

The Artist

Henry Ulke (1821–1910) was ideally situated as a resident of the nation's capital to paint the portraits of government officials. For his last portrait for the secretarial collection, Ulke was able to switch from the copy technique used in his work on his earlier Army portraits and to paint Secretary McCrary—a sitting official—from life. The portrait is signed and dated and brought Ulke the higher fee that had been inaugurated with Huntington's portrait of Alphonso Taft.

GEORGE WASHINGTON McCRARY
Hayes Administration

By Henry Ulke
Oil on canvas, 29½″ x 24½″, 1879

ALEXANDER RAMSEY was born near Harrisburg, Pennsylvania, on 8 September 1815; was orphaned at ten; was employed in a granduncle's store; was a clerk in the office of the register of deeds; studied privately and attended local schools; attended Lafayette College briefly; studied law and was admitted to the bar in 1839; began the practice of law in Harrisburg; was secretary of the state electoral college, 1840; served as chief clerk in the state assembly, 1841; was elected to the U.S. House of Representatives and served from 1843 to 1847; married Anna Jenks, 1845; was chairman of the Whig central committee of Pennsylvania, 1848; was commissioned governor of Minnesota Territory, 1849; ordered a general election and negotiated land treaties with the Sioux; was charged with fraud in the Indian negotiations but was exonerated by the U.S. Senate; retired to private life in St. Paul and became mayor, 1853; was an unsuccessful candidate for governor of Minnesota, 1857; was elected governor in 1859 and reelected in 1861; was elected to the U.S. Senate and served from 1863 to 1875; served as chairman of the Committee on Post Offices and Post Roads; served as Secretary of War, 10 December 1879–5 March 1881; recommended that Congress authorize the position of Assistant Secretary of War; was chairman of the Utah commission appointed to deal with the problem of polygamy, 1881–1886; retired to private life; was president of the Minnesota Historical Society, 1849–1863 and 1891–1903; was president of the Germania Bank of St. Paul, 1889; died in St. Paul, on 22 April 1903.

The Artist

Daniel Huntington (1816–1906) turned to Charles Loring Elliott for his first instruction in art when Elliott, only twenty-one at the time, visited Hamilton College to paint its president while Huntington was a student there. Carried away by the challenge of art, Huntington was soon painting the janitor, his brother, and an imaginary scene from "The Legend of Sleepy Hollow," little realizing that in the future, as a successful artist, he would paint a portrait of the Legend's creator, Washington Irving. Art captured Huntington to such a degree that he left college after a year to devote himself to painting. Huntington painted Secretary Ramsey from life.

ALEXANDER RAMSEY
Hayes Administration

By Daniel Huntington
Oil on canvas, 29½″ x 24½″, 1881

ROBERT TODD LINCOLN was born in Springfield, Illinois, on 1 August 1843; attended local schools and then the Phillips Exeter Academy in New Hampshire; attended Harvard University, 1859–1864; saw his father elected President of the United States, 1861–1865; entered Harvard Law School but left after four months to enter the Army; served on General Grant's staff until the end of the Civil War; studied law in Chicago and was admitted to the bar, 1867; acquired clients among railroad and corporate interests; married Mary Harlan, 1868; was a charter member of the Chicago Bar Association, 1874; was a delegate to the Republican convention of 1880; served as Secretary of War, 5 March 1881–5 March 1885; recommended legislation to prevent and punish white intrusion upon Indian lands; recommended that the Weather Bureau be separated from the Army; recommended an increase in pay for private soldiers as one way to discourage desertion; proposed liberal appropriations to the states to support the formation of volunteer militia organizations; resumed the practice of law, 1885; was recalled to public service as minister to Great Britain and served from 1889 to 1893; resumed his legal practice as counsel to corporate interests including the Pullman Company; became president of the Pullman Company, 1897; resigned in 1911 for reasons of health but continued as chairman of the board; moved to Washington, D.C., 1912, and spent his summers at his Manchester, New Hampshire, estate; died in Washington, D.C., on 26 July 1926.

The Artist

Daniel Huntington (1816–1906) painted President Abraham Lincoln as well as his son, Secretary of War Robert Todd Lincoln. His portrait of Secretary Lincoln was his last contribution to the War Department gallery. He was the first beneficiary of yet another increase in the artist's fee for a secretarial portrait, receiving $750 for the Lincoln image, a scale that would obtain until the turn of the century. Huntington painted Secretary Lincoln from life.

ROBERT TODD LINCOLN
Garfield and Arthur Administrations

By Daniel Huntington
Oil on canvas, 29½″ x 24½″, 1885

WILLIAM CROWNINSHIELD ENDICOTT

was born in Salem, Massachusetts, on 19 November 1826; was educated at Salem Latin School; graduated from Harvard University, 1847; studied law in the office of Nathaniel J. Lord, 1847–1849; attended Harvard Law School, 1849–1850; was admitted to the bar, 1850; with Jairus W. Perry formed the law firm of Perry and Endicott; was a member of the Salem Common Council, 1852, 1853, and 1857, and its president in the latter term; was city solicitor, 1858–1863; married Ellen Peabody, 1859; was defeated for Congress by Benjamin F. Butler in 1879; served as a judge of the Massachusetts Supreme Court, 1873–1882; was an unsuccessful candidate for governor of Massachusetts, 1884; served as Secretary of War, 5 March 1885–5 March 1889; was a key member of the Board on Fortification; proposed that Congress enact legislation requiring that Army officers pass an examination as a condition for promotion; suggested that Congress enact a statute permitting police officers or private citizens to arrest and surrender deserters to military authorities; requested that Congress authorize the publication of the War Department's records by the Public Printer; recommended that the powers of the War and Treasury Departments be clearly defined by legislative act to prevent problems over disbursements; retired from public life to settle in Salem; moved to Boston; was overseer of Harvard College, 1875–1885, president of the Harvard Alumni Association, 1888–1890, and a fellow of the corporation, 1884–1895; was president of the Peabody Academy of Science and the Peabody Education Fund; was a resident member of the Massachusetts Historical Society; died in Boston on 6 May 1900.

The Artist

George Bernard Butler, Jr. (1838–1907), portrait, genre, animal, and still life painter, was born in New York City, where he studied art under Thomas Hicks. In 1859 he went to Paris to study under Thomas Couture, then returned to serve in the military during the Civil War. Despite the loss of his right arm, Butler continued his art career in New York and San Francisco, and was elected a National Academician in 1873. Two years later he returned to Europe and remained in Italy for an extended period. He painted Secretary Endicott from life in 1890.

WILLIAM CROWNINSHIELD ENDICOTT
1st Cleveland Administration

By George Bernard Butler, Jr.
Oil on canvas, 29½″ x 24½″, 1890

REDFIELD PROCTOR was born in Proctorsville, Vermont, on 1 June 1831; was raised by his mother after the early death of his father; received his bachelor's degree from Dartmouth College in 1851 and his advanced degree in 1854; married Emily Dutton, 1858; completed studies at Albany Law School in 1859 and entered practice with a cousin in Boston until the outbreak of the Civil War; enlisted as quartermaster of the 3d Vermont Regiment in 1861; was promoted to major in the 5th Vermont Regiment; contracted tuberculosis and was ordered home in 1862; pursued an outdoor life that restored his health; commanded the 15th Vermont Regiment in the Gettysburg campaign; returned home to form a law partnership in Rutland, Vermont, with Wheelock G. Veazey; was elected to the state legislature, 1867 and 1868; was appointed receiver of a small marble company at Sutherland Falls, 1869; entered the marble business; moved to Sutherland Falls; served in the Vermont Senate, 1874–1875; served as lieutenant governor of Vermont, 1876–1878; served as governor of Vermont, 1878–1880; became president of the Vermont Marble Company, 1880; headed the Vermont delegation to the Republican national convention, 1888; served as Secretary of War, 5 March 1889–5 November 1891; revised the military justice code, instituted a system of efficiency records and promotion examinations for officers, and established a single record and pension division in the department; was elected to the U.S. Senate and served from 1891 until his death in Washington, D.C., on 4 March 1908.

The Artist

Robert Gordon Hardie (1854–1904) was born and died in Brattleboro, Vermont, and was thus a logical choice to paint one of the state's prominent citizens, Secretary Proctor. He studied painting at the Cooper Institute and the National Academy of Design in New York, and under Jean Léon Gerôme in Paris, and was elected to the Society of American Artists in 1879. Hardie painted Secretary Proctor from life shortly after Proctor resigned from the War Department post to succeed George Edmunds in the United States Senate.

REDFIELD PROCTOR
B. Harrison Administration

By Robert Gordon Hardie
Oil on canvas, 29½″ x 24½″, 1892

STEPHEN BENTON ELKINS was born near New Lexington, Perry County, Ohio, on 26 September 1841; moved with his family to Westport, Missouri, in the mid-1840's; graduated from the University of Missouri at Columbia in 1860; taught school in Cass County, Missouri; entered the Union Army as a captain of militia in the 77th Missouri Infantry; with the help of a former student, the future outlaw Cole Younger, escaped from Quantrill's guerrillas; studied law and was admitted to the bar, 1864; crossed the plains to New Mexico, 1864; entered the practice of law at Mesilla; was elected to the territorial legislature, 1864 and 1865; was appointed territorial district attorney, 1866–1867; married Sarah Jacobs, his first wife, 1866; was attorney general of the territory, 1867, and U.S. district attorney, 1867–1870; was elected territorial delegate to the U.S. Congress, 1872, and reelected in 1874, serving to 1877; married his second wife, Hallie Davis, 1875; continued to practice law and founded and was president of the Santa Fe National Bank; pursued broad business interests in land, rail, mining, and finance; moved to Elkins, West Virginia, a town he had founded earlier, to pursue coal and rail interests, circa 1890; served as Secretary of War, 17 December 1891–5 March 1893; recommended that the rank of lieutenant general be revived; recommended increased pay, at least for noncommissioned officers, to improve the quality of the service; broadened the intelligence functions of the Division of Military Information; was elected to the U.S. Senate in 1895, 1901, and 1907, serving until his death in Washington, D.C., on 4 January 1911.

The Artist

Charles Ayer Whipple (1859–1928) was born in Southboro, Massachusetts, and received his major art instruction in Paris under Adolphe Bouguereau, Joseph Fleury, and Gabriel Ferrier. Among his major works are portraits of Presidents William McKinley and Theodore Roosevelt and Generals Nelson A. Miles and Grenville M. Dodge. One of his important commissions, executed in 1919, was to restore the Brumidi-Costaggini mural decorations in the United States Capitol. Whipple painted Secretary Elkins from life in a portrait that differed from the general format of the series.

STEPHEN BENTON ELKINS
B. Harrison Administration

By Charles Ayer Whipple
Oil on canvas, 42½″ x 33½″, 1896

DANIEL SCOTT LAMONT was born on his family's farm in Courtland County, New York, on 9 February 1851; attended Union College at Schenectady, New York, but did not graduate; was employed as engrossing clerk and assistant journal clerk in the state capitol at Albany; was a clerk on the staff of the Democratic state central committee, 1872; was chief clerk of the New York department of state, 1875–1882; was employed on and later acquired a financial interest in the *Albany Argus*, 1877–1882; was assigned by his mentor, Daniel Manning, to New York Governor Grover Cleveland's staff as a political prompter; became private and military secretary with the rank of colonel on the governor's staff, 1883; was appointed private secretary to President Cleveland, 1885; was employed by William C. Whitney in his business ventures, 1889; served as Secretary of War, 5 March 1893–5 March 1897; urged throughout his tenure the adoption of a three-battalion infantry regiment as a part of a general modernization and strengthening of the Army; recommended the construction of a central hall of records to house Army archives; urged that Congress authorize the marking of important battlefields in the manner adopted for Antietam; recommended that lands being used by Apache prisoners at Fort Sill be acquired for their permanent use and their prisoner status be terminated; was vice president of the Northern Pacific Railway Company, 1898–1904; was a director of numerous banks and corporations; died in Millbrook, Dutchess County, New York, on 23 July 1905.

The Artist

Samantha Littlefield Huntley (1865–1949) was born in Watervliet, New York. She studied under John Twachtman and Henry Mowbray at the Art Students League in New York, 1893–1897, then pursued her studies in Paris at the Académie Julien, École des Beaux Arts, and Ecole Normale d'Enseignement du Dessin, 1897–1900. Mrs. Huntley's portrait of Secretary Lamont, executed from a photograph in 1912 some seven years after his death, was presented to the department by Mrs. Lamont with a request that it replace one painted from life by Raimundo de Madrazo, which Mrs. Lamont thought was not a good likeness.

DANIEL SCOTT LAMONT
2d Cleveland Administration

By Samantha Littlefield Huntley
Oil on canvas, 42″ x 29″, 1912

RUSSELL ALEXANDER ALGER was born in Lafayette Township, Medina County, Ohio, on 27 February 1836; was orphaned at twelve and worked on a farm; attended Richfield Academy in Ohio and taught school for two winters; studied law, was admitted to the bar, and began practice in Cleveland, 1859; moved to Grand Rapids, Michigan, 1860; married Annette Henry, 1861; entered the lumber business; enlisted as a private soldier in the Civil War, 1861; was commissioned and served as a captain and major in the 2d Michigan Regiment, as lieutenant colonel in the 6th Michigan, and as colonel of the 5th Michigan; participated in Sheridan's Valley Campaign in Virginia; was brevetted brigadier general and major general of volunteers; settled in Detroit as head of Alger, Smith & Company and the Manistique Lumbering Company; was governor of Michigan, 1885–1886; was elected by his comrades as commander of the Grand Army of the Republic, 1889; served as Secretary of War, 5 March 1897–1 August 1899; recommended that military attachés serving at embassies be given the rank and pay of colonel, and at legations the rank and pay of lieutenant colonel; recommended legislation to authorize a Second Assistant Secretary of War; recommended a constabulary force for Cuba, Puerto Rico, and the Philippines; was criticized for the inadequate preparation and inefficient operation of the department during the Spanish American War; resigned at President McKinley's request, 1899; published *The Spanish-American War*, 1901; was appointed to serve out the unexpired term of the deceased James McMillan in the U.S. Senate, September 1902; was elected in his own right and served in the Senate, 1903–1907; died in Washington, D.C., on 24 January 1907.

The Artist

Percy Ives (1864–1928) was born in Detroit, Michigan. He studied art for four years at the Pennsylvania Academy of Fine Arts and for six years in Paris, France. Among his more important works is his portrait of President Grover Cleveland. He was a member of the Society of Western Artists, and an official of the Detroit Museum of Art and the Archaeological Institute of America. Ives painted Secretary Alger from life soon after Alger's departure from the War Department.

RUSSELL ALEXANDER ALGER
McKinley Administration

By Percy Ives
Oil on canvas, 29½″ x 24½″, 1900

ELIHU ROOT was born in Clinton, Oneida County, New York, on 15 February 1845; graduated from Hamilton College, 1864, and New York University Law School, 1867; was admitted to the bar and after a year with the office of Mann and Parsons opened his own firm with John H. Strahan; married Clara Frances Wales, 1878; was U.S. attorney for the southern district of New York, 1883–1885; was a delegate to the New York State constitutional convention, 1894; served as Secretary of War, 1 August 1899–31 January 1904; was influential in the postwar administration of the former Spanish islands of Puerto Rico, Cuba, and the Philippines; instituted a series of major Army reforms, including a permanent increase in strength, creation of a General Staff, rotation of officers between staff and line, reduced dependency upon seniority, joint planning by Army and Navy, an improved reserve program with special attention to the National Guard, and reorganization of the Army school system; served on the Alaskan Boundary Commission, 1903; served as Secretary of State, 1905–1909; served in the U.S. Senate, 1909–1915; was a member of the Permanent Court of Arbitration at The Hague, 1910; was president of the Carnegie Endowment for International Peace, 1910–1925; was awarded the Nobel Peace Prize, 1912; was president of the New York State constitutional convention, 1915; was head of a special diplomatic mission to Russia, 1917; was a member of the committee of international jurists that planned the Permanent Court of International Justice, 1920; was U.S. commissioner plenipotentiary to the International Conference on the Limitation of Armament, 1921–1922; wrote a number of books on government and international relations; died in New York City on 7 February 1937.

The Artist

Raimundo de Madrazo (1841–1920), portrait and genre painter, was a member of a family of Spanish painters. His grandfather, Jose de Madrazo, was a portrait and historical painter. His father, Federico de Madrazo, also a portrait and historical artist, was Spanish court painter and curator of the Madrid Gallery of Art. Raimundo studied at Rome and at the École des Beaux Arts in Paris, where he eventually established a studio. As an artist of international standing he commanded premium prices for his work. His $2,000 fee for painting Secretary Root from life moved the scale for official portraits beyond the traditional modest progressions and into 20th century levels.

ELIHU ROOT
McKinley and T. Roosevelt Administrations

By Raimundo de Madrazo
Oil on canvas, 31½″ x 25½″, 1907

WILLIAM HOWARD TAFT was born in Cincinnati, Ohio, on 15 September 1857; graduated from Woodward High School, 1874, Yale University, 1878, and Cincinnati Law School, 1880; was admitted to the bar and served as court reporter for the *Cincinnati Commercial*; was assistant prosecuting attorney of Hamilton County, 1881–1883; was assistant solicitor of Hamilton County, 1885–1887; married Helen Herron, 1886; was judge of the superior court, Cincinnati, 1887–1890; was solicitor general of the United States, 1890–1892; was judge of the 6th Judicial Circuit Court, 1892–1900; was professor and dean of the law department, University of Cincinnati, 1896–1900; was president of the Philippine Commission, 1900–1901; became the first civil governor of the Philippine Islands, 1901–1904; declined an appointment to the Supreme Court; served as Secretary of War, 1 February 1904–30 June 1908; began American construction of the Panama Canal and served as conciliator in a threatened upheaval in Cuba; posed the possibility of probationary service for recruits before formal enlistment; directed an investigation into procurement procedures; approved the design of a new Medal of Honor; proposed disposal of small posts and concentration of the Army at brigade posts; was elected President of the United States and served from 1909 to 1913; was defeated by Woodrow Wilson in a reelection bid, 1912; was Kent professor of law at Yale University, 1913–1921; was chairman of the National War Labor Board, 1918; was appointed Chief Justice of the United States Supreme Court, 1921; retired from the bench on 3 February 1930 for reasons of health; died in Washington, D.C., on 8 March 1930.

The Artist

William Valentine Schevill (1864–1951) was born in Cincinnati, Ohio, studied at the School of Design there, and moved on to advanced training under Ludwig von Loeffts in Munich, Germany. He pursued his studies in London, England, and later painted on the Continent as well as in the United States. Schevill painted three portraits of Taft, who was Secretary of War, President of the United States, and Chief Justice of the Supreme Court. The secretarial portrait was painted in Taft's first year as chief executive. Another Taft portrait by Schevill was presented to the National Portrait gallery by the artist's son in 1972.

WILLIAM HOWARD TAFT
T. Roosevelt Administration

By William Valentine Schevill
Oil on canvas, 35″ x 31″, 1909

LUKE EDWARD WRIGHT was born in Giles County, Tennessee, on 29 August 1846; moved with his family to Memphis in 1850; attended the public schools; enlisted at fifteen in the Confederate Army and served with Company G, 154th Senior Tennessee Regiment; was promoted to second lieutenant and cited for bravery under fire in the battle of Murfreesboro, 1863; entered the University of Mississippi, 1867–1868, but did not graduate; married Katherine Semmes, 1868; read law in his father's office, was admitted to the bar, and entered into practice in Memphis; served as attorney general of Tennessee for eight years; was instrumental in establishing a relief committee during an epidemic of yellow fever in 1878; was a member of the second Philippine Commission, 1900; was appointed vice-governor of the Philippines, 1901; was appointed governor general of the Philippines, 1904; served as United States ambassador to Japan, 1906–1907; served as Secretary of War, 1 July 1908–11 March 1909; stressed actions to eliminate unfit officers and sought to take advantage of aviation technology; returned to private life; died in Memphis, Tennessee, on 17 November 1922.

The Artist

Gerard Barry (born 1864) was born in County Cork. Ireland. In 1885 he entered the Académie Julien in Paris, France, where he studied under Jules Lefebvre, Gustave Boulanger, and Carolus Duran. He exhibited in the Paris salons in 1885 and 1886 and at the Royal Academy in London in 1887. In the following year he came to the United States to live permanently except for an eighteen-month visit abroad to study under Carmon. Secretary Wright was still in Washington when Barry painted him from life in 1909. Barry's portrait of House Speaker John White hangs in the U.S. Capitol.

LUKE EDWARD WRIGHT
T. Roosevelt Administration

By Gerard Barry
Oil on canvas, 31½″ x 26½″, 1909

JACOB McGAVOCK DICKINSON was born in Columbus, Mississippi, on 30 January 1851; enlisted at fourteen as a private in the Confederate cavalry; moved with his family to Nashville, Tennessee; graduated from the University of Nashville, 1871, and received his master's degree in 1872; studied law briefly at Columbia University and continued his studies abroad in Leipzig and Paris; was admitted to the Tennessee bar in 1874; married Martha Overton, 1876; was president of the Tennessee Bar Association, 1889–1893; was an assistant attorney general of the United States, 1895–1897; was attorney for the Louisville & Nashville Railroad, 1897–1899; moved to Chicago, Illinois, 1899; became general solicitor for the Illinois Central Railroad, 1899–1901, and general counsel, 1901–1909; was a counsel for the Alaskan Boundary Tribunal, 1903; was president of the American Bar Association, 1907–1908; helped organize the American Society of International Law, served on its executive council from 1907 to 1910, and was its vice president in 1910; served as Secretary of War, 12 March 1909–21 May 1911; proposed legislation to permit the admission of foreign students to West Point; recommended an annuity retirement system for civil service employees; suggested that Congress consider stopping the pay of soldiers rendered unfit for duty because of venereal disease or alcoholism as a means of combatting those problems; was a special assistant attorney general, helped prosecute the U.S. Steel Corporation in 1913, and acted in several important labor cases in 1922; was receiver of the Rock Island Lines, 1915–1917; was president of the Izaak Walton League, 1927–1928; died in Nashville, Tennessee, on 13 December 1928.

The Artist

Ralph Clarkson (1861–1942) was born in Amesbury, Massachusetts, and studied at the Boston Art Museum in the early 1880's before moving to Paris to study under Jules Lefebvre and Gustave Boulanger at the Académie Julien from 1884 to 1887. After a period of portrait painting in New York and a sojourn in Italy, he established a studio in Chicago in 1896, where he became president of the Municipal Art Commission and an instructor and governing member of the Art Institute of Chicago. He served on the art juries of the Paris Exposition (1900), the St. Louis Exposition (1904), and the San Francisco Exposition (1915), and was a founder of Friends of American Art.

JACOB McGAVOCK DICKINSON
Taft Administration

By Ralph Clarkson
Oil on canvas, 29″ x 24″, 1911

HENRY LEWIS STIMSON was born in New York City on 21 September 1867; lost his mother when he was eight and lived with grandparents; was educated at Andover, 1880–1884, Yale University, 1884–1888, and Harvard Law School, 1888–1890; entered the law firm of Root and Clark, 1891; married Mabel Wellington White, 1893; moved up through political circles to a seat on the New York County Republican committee; established a law partnership with Bronson Winthrop, 1899; was U.S. attorney for the southern district of New York, 1906–1909; was an unsuccessful candidate for governor, 1910; served as Secretary of War, 22 May 1911–4 March 1913; enlarged upon troop and administrative reorganizations begun by Secretary Root; sponsored a peacetime Army based upon divisional rather than regimental organization; asserted the authority of the Secretary and the Chief of Staff over bureau heads by relieving The Adjutant General from active duty for insurbordination; ordered troops to the Mexican border, 1913. (For details of Stimson's second term as Secretary of War and his later life, see page 126).

The Artist

Julius Gari Melchers (1860–1932) was born in Detroit, Michigan, and studied art at the Dusseldorf Academy in Germany and under Jules Lefebvre and Gustave Boulanger at the École des Beaux Arts in Paris, France. In addition to portraits, Melchers excelled in religious paintings, mural decorations, and genre pictures, especially of Dutch peasant life. His portrait of Colonel Theodore Roosevelt is in the National Gallery in Washington, D.C.; a mural, "Peace and War," is in the Library of Congress. Melchers's portrait of Secretary Stimson, painted from life, represents a notable departure from traditional style.

HENRY LEWIS STIMSON
Taft Administration

By Julius Gari Melchers
Oil on canvas, 51½″ x 30¾″, 1913

LINDLEY MILLER GARRISON was born in Camden, New Jersey, on 28 November 1864; attended public schools and the Protestant Episcopal Academy in Philadelphia, Pennsylvania; studied at Phillips Exeter Academy for one year before attending Harvard University as a special student, 1884–1885; studied law in the office of Redding, Jones & Carson of Philadelphia; received a law degree from the University of Pennsylvania and was admitted to the bar, 1886; practiced law in Camden, 1888–1898; became a partner in the firm of Garrison, McManus & Enright in Jersey City, 1899; married Margaret Hildeburn, 1900; served as vice-chancellor of New Jersey, 1904–1913, where he came to Governor Woodrow Wilson's notice; served as Secretary of War, 5 March 1913–10 February 1916; directed his efforts towards military preparedness against the background of developing war in Europe and unrest along the Mexican border, proposing a federal reserve force to back up the regular Army; resigned because of differences with President Wilson over military policy; returned to the practice of law in the firm of Hornblower, Miller & Garrison; was appointed receiver of the Brooklyn Rapid Transit Company, December 1918, serving to the end of the receivership in June 1923; died in Seabright, New Jersey, on 19 October 1932.

The Artist

Emil Fuchs (1866–1929), painter and sculptor, was born in Vienna, Austria, and studied at the Imperial Academy of Fine Arts there before going on to study in Berlin. He later taught at the Royal Academy in London and at Paris, Berlin, Munich, Vienna, and Rome before emigrating to the United States in 1905. In 1924 he became a naturalized citizen, and a year later published a memoir, *With Pencil, Brush and Chisel: The Life of an Artist*. Fuchs exhibited at the National Academy of Design in New York, where he made his home, and is represented in the collections of the Metropolitan Museum and Public Library there, as well as in the Library of Congress.

LINDLEY MILLER GARRISON
Wilson Administration

By Emil Fuchs
Oil on canvas, 41¼″ x 34½″, 1917

NEWTON DIEHL BAKER was born in Martinsburg, West Virginia, on 3 December 1871; was educated at Johns Hopkins University, 1888–1892; received a law degree from Washington and Lee University, 1894; entered into practice at Martinsburg, 1894; was secretary to Postmaster General W. L. Wilson, 1896–1897; joined the law firm of Martin G. Foran in Cleveland, Ohio; was assistant director of Cleveland's law department; married Elizabeth Leopold, 1902; was city solicitor of Cleveland, 1902–1912; was mayor of Cleveland, 1912–1916; served as Secretary of War, 9 March 1916–4 March 1921; issued orders for General Pershing's Punitive Expedition into Mexico, 1916; administered the World War I conscription act; chaired the Council of National Defense; adhered rigidly to a policy of professional command free from political intrusion; formalized the "G" sections of the General Staff under the Chief of Staff, refining a concept begun by Secretary Root into a workable pattern that was maintained up to World War II; returned to the private practice of law with the firm of Baker, Hostetler, Sidlo, and Patterson; was appointed a member of the Permanent Court of Arbitration at The Hague, 1928; was a member of the Law Enforcement Commission, 1929; was president of the American Judicature Society and president of the Woodrow Wilson Foundation; died in Cleveland, Ohio, on 25 December 1937.

The Artist

Edmund Hodgson Smart (1873–1942) was born at Ainwick, England. He studied art at the Antwerp Academy in Belgium, at the Académie Julien in Paris, and under Sir Hubert von Herkomer in England. He traveled widely and painted portraits in a number of countries before settling in the United States in 1916. Among his principal portraits are those of England's King Edward VII and Queen Alexandra, American President Warren G. Harding, and three World War I military figures—Marshal Foch, General Pershing, and Admiral Sims. Smart painted Secretary Baker from life in Cleveland in the year Baker left office.

NEWTON DIEHL BAKER
Wilson Administration

By Edmund Hodgson Smart
Oil on canvas, 53½″ x 34½″, 1921

JOHN WINGATE WEEKS was born in Lancaster, New Hampshire, on 11 April 1860; attended local schools and as a teenager taught school for a year; graduated from the United States Naval Academy, 1881; served as a midshipman in the Navy, 1881–1883; married Martha Sinclair, 1885; was assistant land commissioner of the Florida Southern Railway, 1886–1888; moved to Boston to enter the banking and brokerage business; became a partner in the firm of Hornblower and Weeks, 1888–1912; served with the Massachusetts naval militia on coastal patrol during the Spanish American War; retired from the naval reserve as a rear admiral, 1900; was elected alderman of his hometown of Newton, Massachusetts, 1900–1902; was mayor of Newton, 1903–1904; served as chairman of the state Republican convention, 1905; served in the U.S. House of Representatives, 1905–1913; was appointed by the state legislature to fill the U.S. Senate seat of Winthrop M. Crane, and served from 1913 to 1919; was a member of the military affairs committee; was a candidate for the Republican nomination for president, 1916; served as Secretary of War, 5 March 1921–13 October 1925; supervised the final transition from a wartime to a peacetime footing; established the Army Industrial College at Ft. McNair, 1923; appeared before Congress to defend the adequacy of U.S. air defenses against charges advanced by General Billy Mitchell; urged congressional authorization for special promotions of outstanding officers, not to exceed two percent of the number promoted on the basis of seniority; resigned the Army secretaryship because of ill health, 1925; died at Mount Prospect, Lancaster, New Hampshire, on 12 July 1926.

The Artist

Arthur Merton Hazard (1872–1930) was born in North Bridgewater, Massachusetts. He studied initially at the Museum of Fine Arts and the Cowles Art School in Boston before going to Europe to study under a number of leading instructors in Paris. He was best known for his war pictures which are included in the collections of the National Gallery of Art and the American Red Cross in Washington, Temple Israel in Boston, and the Canadian Houses of Parliament in Ottawa. Hazard, who made his home in Hollywood, California, died while on a visit to France. He painted Secretary Weeks in the brief interval between the Army official's resignation and his death.

JOHN WINGATE WEEKS
Harding and Coolidge Administrations

By Arthur Merton Hazard
Oil on canvas, 41½″ x 32½″, 1926

DWIGHT FILLEY DAVIS was born in St. Louis, Missouri, on 5 July 1879; attended Smith Academy in St. Louis; graduated from Harvard University, 1900; established the Davis Cup as a trophy for excellence in international tennis competition; received a law degree from Washington University of St. Louis, 1903; became active in civic affairs; was a member of the public library board, 1904–1907, and the board of control of the Museum of Fine Arts, 1904–1907 and 1911–1912; married Helen Brooks, 1905; was a member of the house of delegates of the city government, 1907–1909, a member of the board of freeholders, 1909–1911, and chairman of the City Planning Commission, 1911–1915, and concurrently city park commissioner; exercised his special interest in recreational facilities by developing golf courses, baseball fields, and the first municipal tennis courts in the United States; served on the executive committee of the National Municipal League, 1908–1912; attended the Plattsburg Military Camp for businessmen, 1915; was a member of the Rockefeller War Relief Committee, 1916–1917; entered military service and participated in the St. Mihiel and Meuse-Argonne operations with the 138th Infantry Regiment, 35th Division; became director of the War Finance Corporation; was Assistant Secretary of War, 1923–1924; served as Secretary of War, 14 October 1925–5 March 1929; superintended the Army's first experiments with a mechanized force; was governor general of the Philippines, 1929–1932; following the death of his first wife, married Pauline Morton Sabin, 1936; was director general of the Army Specialist Corps, 1942; died in Washington, D.C., on 28 November 1945.

The Artist

Douglas Chandor (1897–1953) was born in Woldingham, Surrey, England, and studied art at the Slade School in London. He served with the British Army throughout World War I and was disabled and discharged in 1918. The following year he took up portrait painting and within three years had his first exhibit at the Royal Academy in London. In the early 1920's he painted a series of portraits of the former prime ministers of the British Empire, and in 1926 he painted Queen Marie of Rumania. Chandor moved to the United States in 1926 and began to paint notable Americans, including Secretaries of War Davis and Good.

DWIGHT FILLEY DAVIS
Coolidge Administration

By Douglas Chandor
Oil on canvas, 35½″ x 27½″, 1929

JAMES WILLIAM GOOD was born in Cedar Rapids, Iowa, on 24 September 1866; graduated from Coe College, Iowa, 1892; studied law at the University of Michigan Law School and received his degree in 1893; was admitted to the bar in the same year; practiced briefly in Indiana then returned to Cedar Rapids to form a partnership with Charles J. Deccon; was city attorney of Cedar Rapids, 1906–1908; was a member of the U.S. House of Representatives from 1909 to 1921, was chairman of the Appropriations Committee, 1919–1921, and had a substantial part in the establishment of the national budget system; resigned in 1921 to return to the practice of the law in Evanston, Illinois, as a partner in the firm of Good, Childs, Bobb & Wescott; served as western campaign manager for Calvin Coolidge in 1924 and Herbert Hoover in 1928; served as Secretary of War, 6 March–18 November 1929; died while in office in Washington, D.C., on 18 November 1929.

The Artist

Douglas Chandor (1897–1953) established homes in New York City and Weatherford, Texas, after moving to the United States from his native England in 1926, and quickly developed a successful portrait business with a number of prominent Americans as his subjects. He painted President Hoover, Vice President Curtis, and the entire Hoover cabinet including Secretary Good in 1929. Among his later subjects were President and Mrs. Franklin D. Roosevelt, House Speaker Sam Rayburn, Bernard Baruch, and Andrew Mellon. In 1946, Chandor painted Winston Churchill and Mrs. Churchill at a moment when the wartime leader, no longer Prime Minister, was launching his six-volume, Nobel Prize-winning memoir.

JAMES WILLIAM GOOD
Hoover Administration

By Douglas Chandor
Oil on canvas, 35¼″ x 27¼″, 1929

PATRICK JAY HURLEY was born in the Choctaw Nation, Indian Territory, on 8 January 1883; graduated from Indian University (now Bacone College), 1905; received a law degree from the National University of Law, Washington, D.C., in 1908, and from George Washington University, Washington, D.C., in 1913; was admitted to the bar and commenced practice at Tulsa, Oklahoma, 1908; was admitted to the bar of the Supreme Court, 1912; was national attorney for the Choctaw Nation, 1912–1917; served in the Indian Territorial Volunteer Militia, 1902–1907, and the Oklahoma National Guard, 1914–1917; served with the American Expeditionary Forces (AEF) in the Aisne-Marne, Meuse-Argonne, and St. Mihiel operations, rising to lieutenant colonel, and negotiated the access agreement between the AEF and the Grand Duchy of Luxembourg, 1919; married Ruth Wilson, 1919; served as Assistant Secretary of War, March-December 1929; served as Secretary of War, 9 December 1929–3 March 1933; supervised Army activities to alleviate the effects of the depression, 1930–1931; urged an increase in pay and recommended the enactment of comprehensive promotion legislation for the Army; issued the executive order to Chief of Staff General MacArthur to evict the Bonus Army from Washington, 1932; was called to active duty as a brigadier general and served on a special mission to Australia and as the first U.S. minister to New Zealand, 1942; was a personal representative of the President of the United States to the Soviet Union, 1942, and to the nations of the Near East and Middle East, 1943; was a presidential emissary and then ambassador to China, 1943–1944; was promoted to major general, 1944; returned to private interests in New Mexico; died in Santa Fe, New Mexico, on 30 July 1963.

The Artist

Frank Townsend Hutchens (1869–1937) was born in Canandaigua, New York, and studied art at the Art Students League in New York City and at the Académie Colorossi and Académie Julien in Paris, France. He exhibited at the Royal Academy in London, the Paris Salon, and the Amsterdam International Exhibition as well as at the National Academy of Design in New York and numerous galleries in major cities around the United States. Hutchens divided his time between homes in Norwalk, Connecticut, and Taos, New Mexico, and it was the latter connection that brought him to Secretary Hurley's attention as a portraitist.

PATRICK JAY HURLEY
Hoover Administration

By Frank Townsend Hutchens
Oil on canvas, 35¼″ x 29½″, 1932

GEORGE HENRY DERN was born near Scribner, Dodge County, Nebraska, on 8 September 1872; attended the public schools and graduated from Fremont Normal College, Fremont, Nebraska, in 1888; attended the University of Nebraska, 1893–1894; moved with his family to Salt Lake City, Utah, 1894; entered the mining field, rising through successive levels in the Mercur Gold Mining and Milling Company to become general manager after a merger of several firms into the Consolidated Mercur Gold Mines Company, 1894–1901; was instrumental in the development of several important mining processes, including the Holt-Dern roaster oven; was a Utah state senator, 1914–1923, and sponsored much forward-looking legislation; was governor of Utah, 1925–1932, and instituted a notable tax revision program; was chairman of the National Governors' Conference, 1930; served as Secretary of War, 4 March 1933–27 August 1936; supervised the Army's participation in the New Deal's Civilian Conservation Corps program, and inaugurated important Army engineer public works water projects; urged construction of a new building to house the War Department; appointed the Baker Board on Army aviation and approved its recommendation for procurement of 2,320 planes in three years; recommended that Congress authorize a policy of training at least 30,000 reserve officers annually for two-week periods; died while in office in Washington, D.C., on 27 August 1936.

The Artist

Albert Salzbrenner (born 1865) was born in Dresden, Germany, and studied painting at the Royal Academy there under Leon Pohle and Ludwig von Hoffman. He followed this with two years of study in Paris under Carolus Duran, and one each in Munich and Vienna, the latter under Heinrich von Angeli. After two years in Rome studying the old masters, he had his first exhibition in Paris in 1888. Salzbrenner painted a few portraits during a visit to the United States, and, finding his interest captured, he soon returned to settle eventually at Winston-Salem, North Carolina. Among his other works are portraits of Joseph Smith of the Mormon Church, Governor William Spry of Utah, and Secrerary Dern's parents.

GEORGE HENRY DERN
F. Roosevelt Administration

By Albert Salzbrenner
Oil on canvas, 39¼″ x 29¼″, 1934

HARRY HINES WOODRING was born in Elk City, Kansas, on 31 May 1890; was educated in city and county schools; at sixteen began work as a janitor in the First National Bank of Neodesha, Kansas; moved up to become vice president and owner of the bank; enlisted as a private and was later commissioned as a second lieutenant in the Tank Corps in World War I; was elected department commander of the American Legion in Kansas, 1928; sold his banking business to enter politics, 1929; was elected governor of Kansas, 1931, and served to 1933; married Helen Coolidge, 1933; served as Assistant Secretary of War, 6 April 1933–25 September 1936, with supervision over procurement matters; served as Secretary of War, 25 September 1936–20 June 1940; projected the recommendations of his predecessor for increasing the strength of the Regular Army, National Guard, and Reserve Corps; directed a revision of mobilization plans to bring personnel and procurement into balance; stressed the need to perfect the initial (peacetime) protective force; returned to private life; ran unsuccessfully for governor of Kansas, 1946, and for the Democratic nomination for that post, 1956; died at Topeka, Kansas, on 9 September 1967.

The Artist

Tino Costa (1892–1947) had a varied career as a portraitist, painting subjects as diverse as King Christian of Denmark and child movie star Shirley Temple. He painted two U.S. Presidents, Herbert C. Hoover and Franklin D. Roosevelt, and General Douglas MacArthur. Costa was living in California at the time of his death, some seven years after he painted Secretary Woodring.

HARRY HINES WOODRING
F. Roosevelt Administration

By Tino Costa
Oil on canvas, 29½″ x 24½″, 1940

HENRY LEWIS STIMSON was a delegate at large to the New York State constitutional convention, 1915; entered upon active Reserve service as a major in the Judge Advocate General's department, 1917; became a lieutenant colonel in the 305th Field Artillery, August 1917; served with American forces in France, December 1917–August 1918; became colonel of the 31st Field Artillery, August 1918; returned to his legal career; was commissioned colonel in the Organized Reserve Corps in 1921 and brigadier general in 1922; was a presidential emissary to Nicaragua, 1927; was governor general of the Philippines, 1927–1929; served as Secretary of State, 28 March 1929–4 March 1933; was chairman of the American delegation to the London Naval Conference, 1930; returned to private life; served again as Secretary of War, 10 July 1940–21 September 1945; presided over the expansion of the War Department and the Army to meet the World War II emergency; was a leader in seeking the enactment of legislation for compulsory conscription, 1940; was closely involved in the decisions to evacuate Japanese Americans and aliens from coastal regions, 1941–1942, and to use the atomic bomb, 1945; retired to his Long Island estate where he died on 20 October 1950. (For details of his earlier life, see page 108.)

The Artist

Fred W. Wright (born 1880) studied at the Art Students League in New York and the Académie Julien in Paris before embarking upon a career as a portrait painter in New York. His work is represented in a number of collections around the country. Robert Brackman (1898–　) was born in Odessa, Russia, came to the United States in 1908, studied at the National Academy of Design, and in the 1930's joined the faculties of the Art Students League and the Brooklyn Institute of Art. His work is represented in numerous collections. Brackman's original portrait of Secretary Stimson is in the Skull and Bones Club at Yale University; Mr. Stimson privately commissioned the Wright copy for the Army gallery.

HENRY LEWIS STIMSON
F. Roosevelt Administration

By Fred W. Wright after Robert Brackman
Oil on canvas, 39½″ x 33½″, 1945

ROBERT PORTER PATTERSON was born in Glens Falls, New York, on 12 February 1891; graduated from Union College, Schenectady, New York, 1912; received a law degree from Harvard University, 1915; entered practice in New York City in Elihu Root's firm; served as a private with New York's Seventh Regiment on the Mexican Border, 1916; entered upon active duty as a second lieutenant at the Reserve Officers' Training Camp, Plattsburg, New York, 1917; was promoted to captain and then major with the 306th Infantry of the American Expeditionary Forces in France, receiving the Distinguished Service Cross for heroism in action, 1918; returned to his law career and established a successful new firm in New York; married Margaret Winchester, 1920; was appointed judge for the southern district court of New York, 1930; was promoted to the second circuit court of appeals, 1939; was appointed Assistant Secretary of War, July 1940, and advanced to Under Secretary, December 1940; had statutory responsibility for production and procurement and was the Army representative on the War Production Board, the War Manpower Commission, and the Committee for Congested Production; was appointed Secretary of War and served from 27 September 1945 to 18 July 1947; pressed for unification of the armed services and a single Chief of Staff; returned to the practice of law in the firm of Patterson, Belknap, and Webb; was president of the Bar Association of the City of New York, president of the Council on Foreign Relations, and president of Freedom House; died in a plane crash at Elizabeth, New Jersey, on 22 January 1952.

The Artist

Joseph Cummings Chase (1878–1965) was born at Kents Hill, Maine, and studied art at the Pratt Institute in New York and the Pennsylvania Academy of Fine Arts before going on to study under Jean Paul Laurens at the Académie Julien in Paris. He painted military figures from both World Wars—soldiers cited for bravery as well as senior commanders—and various prominent personalities, such as Albert Einstein, Will Rogers, Theodore Roosevelt, and Al Smith. Many of his portraits appeared as illustrations in his two books, *My Friends Look Better Than Ever* (1950) and *Face Value* (1962).

ROBERT PORTER PATTERSON
Truman Administration

By Joseph Cummings Chase
Oil on canvas, 35½″ x 27½″, ca. 1947

Secretaries of the Army

KENNETH CLAIBORNE ROYALL was born in Goldsboro, North Carolina, on 24 July 1894; graduated from the University of North Carolina, 1914; was admitted to the North Carolina bar, 1916; attended Harvard University Law School and received his degree, 1917; married Margaret Best, 1917; served in France as a second lieutenant in the 317th Army Field Artillery, 1918–1919; was commissioned a captain in the North Carolina National Guard and organized a Field Artillery battery, 1921; resumed the practice of law in Raleigh and Goldsboro, North Carolina; served in the state senate, 1927; was president of the North Carolina Bar Association, 1929–1930; was a presidential elector, 1940; was commissioned a colonel, 1942, and appointed chief of the legal section, fiscal division, Headquarters, Services of Supply (later Army Service Forces); received presidential appointment to defend before the Supreme Court the German saboteurs who entered the United States clandestinely; was promoted to brigadier general and appointed deputy fiscal director of Army Service Forces; was special assistant to the Secretary of War, April–November 1945; served as Under Secretary of War, 9 November 1945–18 July 1947; served as the last Secretary of War, 19 July–17 September 1947; supervised the separation of the Department of the Air Force from the Department of the Army; became first Secretary of the Army when National Defense Act of 1947 took effect, 17 September 1947–27 April 1949; was the last Army secretary to hold the cabinet status, which was henceforth assigned to the Secretary of Defense; returned to the practice of law in New York City; was a delegate at large to the Democratic National Convention, 1964; died in Durham, North Carolina, on 25 May 1971.

The Artist

Alfred Jonniaux (1882–1974) was born in Brussels, Belgium, and studied at the Athenée d'Ixelles and the Académie des Beaux Arts there. He established studios in London and Paris and painted the portraits of various representatives of European royalty, also specializing in character studies and landscapes. Jonniaux fled the Nazi occupation of Western Europe and became a naturalized American citizen in 1946. He established studios in San Francisco and Washington and painted portraits of many prominent figures, including Kenneth Royall, the last Secretary of War and the first Secretary of the Army.

KENNETH CLAIBORNE ROYALL
Truman Administration

By Alfred Jonniaux
Oil on canvas, 49½″ x 39½″, ca. 1949

GORDON GRAY was born in Baltimore, Maryland, on 30 May 1909; graduated from the University of North Carolina, 1930; received a degree from the Yale Law School, 1933; was admitted to the New York bar and entered into practice there, 1933–1935; was admitted to the North Carolina bar and practiced there, 1935–1937; was president of the Piedmont Publishing Company, publishers of the *Winston-Salem Journal* and the *Twin City Sentinel* and operator of radio station WSJS, 1937–1947; married Jane Boyden Craige, 1938 (deceased 1953); served in the state senate, 1939–1942; entered military service as a private, 1942, was commissioned in Infantry, 1943, served overseas with Headquarters, Twelfth Army Group, 1944–1945, and emerged as a captain; was again a state senator, 1945–1947; served as Assistant Secretary of the Army, 24 September 1947–27 April 1949, and as Under Secretary of the Army, 25 May–19 June 1949; served as Secretary of the Army, 20 June 1949–12 April 1950; supervised the phaseout of Selective Service inductees and terminated the Army's military government operation in Germany, 1949–1950; was a special assistant to the President on foreign economic policy, 1950; served as president of the University of North Carolina, 1950–1955; was Assistant Secretary of Defense for International Security Affairs, 1955–1957; married Nancy McGuire Beebe, 1956; was director of the Office of Defense Mobilization, 1957–1958; was special assistant to the President for National Security Affairs, 1958–1961; was awarded the Presidential Medal of Freedom, 1961; was a member of the President's Foreign Intelligence Advisory Board, 1961–1977, and chairman of the board of Triangle Broadcasting Company, 1969–1975; was chairman of the board of Summit Communications, Inc.; died in Washington, D.C., on 26 November 1982.

The Artist

Adrian Lamb (1901–   ) studied at the Art Students League in New York and the Académie Julien in Paris. He lives in Connecticut and has a studio in New York City where he paints prominent Americans of the past and present. Gardner Cox (1906–   ) studied at the Art Students League and at Harvard University and the Boston Museum of Fine Arts. He lives in Cambridge and has a studio in Boston where he paints prominent Americans. Secretary Gray owned the original Cox portrait; he privately commissioned the Lamb copy and placed it in the Army gallery.

GORDON GRAY
Truman Administration

By Adrian Lamb after Gardner Cox
Oil on canvas, 39½″ x 29½″, 1953

FRANK PACE, JR., was born in Little Rock, Arkansas, on 5 July 1912; attended local schools and then the Hill School, Pottstown, Pennsylvania; graduated from Princeton University, 1933; received a new degree from Harvard University, 1936; was admitted to the Arkansas bar and practiced law there, 1936–1942; was assistant district attorney of the Twelfth Judicial District, 1936–1938; was general attorney, Arkansas Revenue Department, 1938–1940; married Margaret Janney, 1940; entered the Army as a second lieutenant, 1942; served in the Air Transport Command, Army Air Corps, and emerged as a major, 1945; was a special assistant to the Attorney General, U.S. Taxation Division, 1946; was executive assistant to the Postmaster General, 1946–1948; was assistant director, 1948, then director, 1949–1950, of the Bureau of the Budget; served as Secretary of the Army, 12 April 1950–20 January 1953; executed the structural and functional changes mandated by the Army Organization Act of 1950 and headed the Army during the Korean War, 1950–1953; implemented policies to broaden the Army's utilization of Negro manpower; elevated research and development to the Deputy Chief of Staff level; was chairman of the Defense Ministers Conference, North Atlantic Treaty Organization (NATO), 1950; was chairman of the American Council of NATO, 1957–1960; was vice chairman, President's Commission on National Goals, 1959–1960; was a member of the President's Foreign Intelligence Advisory Board, 1961-1973; was chairman of the board, Corporation for Public Broadcasting, 1968–1972; was a member and past president of the National Institute of Social Sciences and a member of the Brookings Institution; died in Greenwich, Connecticut, on 8 January 1988.

The Artist

Germain Green Glidden (1913–), portraitist, muralist, and cartoonist, was a fine arts major at Harvard University, attended the Art Students League in New York City, and studied life drawing, painting, and the old masters under Alexander Abels and sculpture under Mahonri Young. Included among his several hundred portraits are those of Secretary of the Army Pace and Secretary of the Air Force Donald Quarles. Glidden maintains a studio in Norwalk, Connecticut, and is founder, president, and chairman of the National Art Museum of Sport in Madison Square Garden Center in New York City.

FRANK PACE, JR.
Truman Administration

By Germain Green Glidden
Oil on composition board, 41½″ x 35½″, 1952

ROBERT TEN BROECK STEVENS was born in Fanwood, New Jersey, on 31 July 1899; was graduated from Phillips Andover, 1917; interrupted his education to serve as a second lieutenant of Field Artillery in World War I, 1918; graduated from Yale University, 1921; joined the textile firm of J. P. Stevens Company, 1921; married Dorothy Goodwin Whitney, 1923; was president of J. P. Stevens Company, 1929–1942; was an administrative representative in the industrial section of the National Recovery Administration, 1933; was Class B director of the Federal Reserve Bank of New York, 1934–1955, and Class C director and chairman, 1948–1953; attended a special civilian course at the Command and General Staff School, Fort Leavenworth, 1941; entered upon active duty with the Army as a lieutenant colonel, 1942, was promoted to colonel, and served to 1945 in the Office of the Quartermaster General's procurement division, with a period of temporary duty in the European Theater; returned to J. P. Stevens Company as chairman of the board, 1945–1953; was chairman of the Business Advisory Council, U.S. Department of Commerce, 1951–1952; served as Secretary of the Army, 4 February 1953–21 July 1955; supervised the post–Korean War retrenchment; proposed advance security clearances for key industrial facilities to enable them to operate immediately in an emergency; defended the Army against reckless charges advanced by Senator Joseph R. McCarthy of Wisconsin in Congressional (Army-McCarthy) hearings held to investigate Communist influence in government, 1953–1954; returned to the J. P. Stevens Company as president, 1955–1959, and served as chairman of the executive committee, 1969–1974; died in Edison, New Jersey, on 31 January 1983.

The Artist

Thomas Edgar Stephens (1886–1966) was born in England and studied art at Cardiff University in Wales, the Heatherly School in London, and the Académie Julien in Paris. He was already a trained artist when he moved to the United States in 1929 to settle in New York and become an American citizen. Between 1946 and 1960 he painted twenty-four portraits of Dwight D. Eisenhower for various institutions and individuals, and it was Stephens who painted the entire Eisenhower cabinet and later induced the former president to take up painting as a hobby. He also painted the last life portrait of Winston Churchill as prime minister.

ROBERT TEN BROECK STEVENS
Eisenhower Administration

By Thomas Edgar Stephens
Oil on canvas, 41½″ x 33½″, ca. 1955

WILBER MARION BRUCKER was born in Saginaw, Michigan, on 23 June 1894; graduated from the University of Michigan, 1916; enlisted in the Michigan National Guard and served with its 33d Infantry Regiment on the Mexican Border, 1916–1917; attended the First Officers' Training Camp, Fort Sheridan, Illinois, and was commissioned a second lieutenant of Infantry; served in France with the 166th Infantry, 42d Division, in the Chateau Thierry, St. Mihiel, and Meuse-Argonne operations, 1917–1918; was assistant prosecuting attorney of Saginaw County, Michigan, 1919–1923, and prosecuting attorney, 1923–1927; married Clara Hantel, 1923; was assistant attorney general of Michigan, 1927–1928, and attorney general, 1928–1930; was governor of Michigan, 1930–1932; was a captain in the Officer Reserve Corps, 1922–1937; was a member of the law firm of Clark, Klein, Brucker, and Waples, 1937–1954; served as general counsel of the Department of Defense, 1954–1955; served as Secretary of the Army, 21 July 1955–19 January 1961; administered the Army during a period of major technological advance, especially in the missile-satellite field, and at a time when the Army's place in the national defense structure was overshadowed by a "massive retaliation" philosophy; under his direction the Army instituted a five-element (pentagonal) organization concept for the division, established a Strategic Army Corps for emergency reaction, and launched the Free World's first satellite; returned to legal practice in Detroit in the firm of Brucker and Brucker, 1961–1968; was a member of the Board of Directors of Freedoms Foundation; died at Grosse Pointe Farms, Michigan, on 28 December 1968.

The Artist

Charles J. Fox is the pseudonym of Leo Fox, a New York City entrepreneur who for many years commissioned portraits of leading figures in government, business, society, and the professions. The portraits, signed C. J. Fox, were executed by New York artist Irving Resnikoff (born 1897) during a forty-year association with Fox. The Army gallery contains three C. J. Fox portraits—those of Secretaries Brucker, Stahr, and Ailes.

WILBER MARION BRUCKER
Eisenhower Administration

By Irving Resnikoff, signed C.J. Fox
Oil on canvas, 44½″ x 31½″, ca. 1961

ELVIS JACOB STAHR, JR., was born in Hickman, Kentucky, on 9 March 1916; was graduated from the University of Kentucky, 1936, and was Cadet Colonel of its ROTC regiment; studied law on a Rhodes Scholarship at Oxford University, England, 1936–1939, and received three degrees; became an associate in the New York law firm of Mudge, Stern, Williams & Tucker, 1939; was called to active duty as a second lieutenant, Infantry, October 1941, and served as weapons instructor at the Infantry School, Fort Benning, Georgia, 1942–1943; was an officer student at Yale University, 1943, and received a diploma in Chinese language; served in North Africa, 1943, and in the Chinese Combat Command, China-Burma-India Theater, 1944–1945; was awarded the Bronze Star Medal with Oak Leaf Cluster (U.S.) and three Republic of China decorations; left service as a lieutenant colonel, December 1945; returned to his law firm and married Dorothy Berkfield, 1946; was professor of law and dean of the College of Law at the University of Kentucky, 1948–1956; was Special Assistant to the Secretary of the Army for Reserve Forces, 1951–1953; was vice chancellor of the University of Pittsburgh, 1957–1958; was president of West Virginia University, 1958–1961; served as Secretary of the Army, 24 January 1961–30 June 1962; under his direction a major Army reorganization plan was launched, the combat division structure reorganized, special warfare forces expanded, the community relations (civic action) role enlarged, and the Army strengthened during the Berlin crisis; was president of Indiana University, 1962–1968; was president of the National Audubon Society, 1968–1979, and senior counselor, 1979–1981; since 1982 has been the Washington partner of the San Francisco law firm of Chickering & Gregory, P.C.; has been a member of the U.S. delegation to four international conferences; has served on four Presidential Commissions; was president of the Association of the United States Army, 1965–1968, and chairman, 1969–1974; was national chairman of the USO, 1973–1976; holds twenty-seven honorary doctoral degrees.

The Artist

New York entrepreneur Leo Fox supplied portraits of Secretaries Brucker and Ailes as well as that of Secretary Stahr under the Charles J. Fox pseudonym. Others of his commissions included President John F. Kennedy, Vice President Alben W. Barkley, Federal Bureau of Investigation Director J. Edgar Hoover, and Selective Service Director Lewis B. Hershey. Fox retained the services of Irving Resnikoff to paint portraits for which he was the contracting agent.

ELVIS JACOB STAHR, JR.
Kennedy Administration

By Irving Resnikoff, signed C.J. Fox
Oil on canvas, 44½″ x 34½″, ca. 1962

CYRUS ROBERTS VANCE was born in Clarksburg, West Virginia, on 27 March 1917; attended the Kent School in Connecticut; graduated from Yale University in 1939 and received his law degree there in 1942; enlisted in the U.S. Navy V–7 program as a midshipman, 1942, and graduated as an ensign in the Naval Reserve; became an instructor in naval ordnance at Prairie State Midshipman's School, New York City, 1942–1943; served on destroyers in the Atlantic and Pacific regions, 1943–1946, completing duty as a lieutenant; became assistant to the president of the Mead Corporation, 1946–1947; married Grace Elsie Sloan, 1947; entered the practice of law with the New York firm of Simpson, Thacher & Bartlett, 1947, and became a partner in 1956; was special counsel to the Preparedness Investigating Subcommittee of the Senate Armed Services Committee, 1957–1960, and consulting counsel to the Special Committee on Space and Astronautics, 1958; was general counsel of the Department of Defense, 1961–1962; served as Secretary of the Army, 5 July 1962–21 January 1964; under his direction the major reorganization of 1962 was implemented, the Army went on alert during the Cuban crisis, the Reserve Components were realigned, and the Army provided troops in support of civil authorities during the integration of universities in Mississippi and Alabama; served as Deputy Secretary of Defense, 1964–1967; was special representative of the President of the United States to Cyprus, 1967, and to Korea, 1968; was chief U.S. negotiator at the Paris Peace Conference on Vietnam, 1968–1969; was awarded the Presidential Medal of Freedom, 1969; returned to the practice of law in New York City; served as Secretary of State, 1977–1980; resumed the practice of law with the firm of Simpson, Thacher & Bartlett; became chairman of the Federal Reserve Bank of New York in 1989 and cochairman of the Financial Services Volunteer Corps, a Department of State/Agency for International Development project, in 1990.

The Artist

George Augusta (1922–   ) was born in Boston, Massachusetts, and became interested in painting while serving with the United States Army's signal intelligence service in Italy in World War II. He took advantage of his situation to study art in Florence, Italy, then returned to Boston to study privately with Ernest Lee Major from 1946 until the latter's death in 1950. In addition to his portrait of Secretary Vance, Augusta also painted Secretaries Resor and Callaway for the gallery.

CYRUS ROBERTS VANCE
Kennedy and L. Johnson Administrations

By George Augusta
Oil on canvas, 41½″ x 33½″, 1970

STEPHEN AIILES was born in Romney, West Virginia, on 25 May 1912; attended Episcopal High School, Alexandria, Virginia, 1929; graduated from Princeton University, 1933; received his law degree from West Virginia University, 1936; was admitted to the West Virginia bar, 1936; was assistant professor of law, West Virginia University, 1937–1940; married Helen Wales, 1939; practiced law at Martinsburg, 1940–1942; was a member of the legal staff of the Office of Price Administration, 1942–1946, and its general counsel, 1945–1946; served as counsel to the American Economic Mission to Greece, 1947, which preceded the Truman Doctrine aid to Greece and Turkey; returned to private law practice with the Washington firm of Steptoe & Johnson, 1948–1949; was legal consultant to the director of the Office of Price Stabilization, 1951; served as Under Secretary of the Army, 9 February 1961–28 January 1964; served as Secretary of the Army, 28 January 1964–1 July 1965; under his direction the Army dealt with riots in the Panama Canal Zone in which the Secretary helped negotiate a settlement, provided disaster assistance following earthquakes in Skopje, Yugoslavia, and Anchorage, Alaska, made an agreement with the Federal Republic of Germany to develop jointly a new main battle tank, assumed responsibility for the nation's Civil Defense function, provided troops to protect American personnel and bring an end to a civil war in the Dominican Republic, and dispatched the first combat units to Vietnam; returned to legal practice; was a director of the Panama Canal Company, 1966–1970; was president of the Association of American Railroads, 1971–1977; resumed the practice of law.

The Artist

In addition to portraits of three Army Secretaries, New York entrepreneur Leo Fox contracted for and Irving Resnikoff painted the portraits of Chief Justice Harlan F. Stone of the Supreme Court, Chairmen Clarence Cannon and George H. Mahon of the House Appropriations Committee, and J. George Stewart, Architect of the Capitol. The C. J. Fox signature also appears on the portraits of a number of figures in the business world, including J. Paul Austin of the Coca Cola Company, Harold S. Geneen of International Telephone and Telegraph Company, A. P. Giannini of the Bank of America, and V. J. Skutt of Mutual of Omaha.

STEPHEN AILES
L. Johnson Administration

By Irving Resnikoff, signed C.J. Fox
Oil on canvas, 44½″ x 34½″, ca. 1965

STANLEY ROGERS RESOR was born in New York City on 5 December 1917; attended the Groton School, Groton Connecticut; graduated from Yale University, 1939; entered Yale Law School; married Jane Lawler Pillsbury, 1942; was commissioned a second lieutenant of Field Artillery from the Yale ROTC course, 1942; entered upon active duty and served with the 10th Armored Division in the United States, 1942–1944, and overseas, 1944–1945, in combat in the European Theater; received the Silver Star, the Bronze Star, and the Purple Heart; was separated from the service as a lieutenant colonel and returned to Yale Law School to complete his studies and receive his law degree, 1946; was admitted to the New York bar, 1946; entered into practice as an associate and then partner in the New York firm of Deveboise, Plimpton, Lyons, and Gates, 1946–1965, specializing in corporate law; served as Under Secretary of the Army, 5 April–1 July 1965; served as Secretary of the Army, 2 July 1965–30 June 1971; during his tenure major forces were committed to Vietnam at presidential direction, the Army's first airmobile division was fielded, the American line of communications in Europe was shifted from France to Germany and the Benelux countries, Army forces were committed in support of civil authorities in serious civil disturbances, Vietnamization of the war in Southeast Asia was accelerated and withdrawal of Army forces instituted, and the Army initiated actions to achieve an all-volunteer force; returned to the practice of law in New York; was United States representative with the rank of ambassador to the Mutual and Balanced Force Reduction negotiations in Vienna, Austria, 1973–1978; was awarded the George C. Marshall Medal from the Association of the United States Army, 1974; was appointed Under Secretary of Defense for Policy, August 1978; resigned and returned to private life, March 1979; received the Sylvanius Thayer Award from the Association of West Point Graduates in 1984.

The Artist

George Augusta (1922–   ) is a native Bostonian who studied art in Boston and in Italy and maintains a studio in Hampton Falls, New Hampshire. He has painted the portraits of a number of individuals prominent in business, the professions, and government, and is represented in the Army's gallery with his portraits of Secretaries Vance, Resor, and Callaway.

148

STANLEY ROGERS RESOR
L. Johnson and Nixon Administrations

By George Augusta
Oil on canvas, 39½″ x 31¾″, 1971

ROBERT FREDERICK FROEHLKE was born in Neenah, Wisconsin, on 15 October 1922; attended high school at Marshfield, Wisconsin; enlisted in the U.S. Army in 1943, served in the Infantry in the European Theater, and left the service as a captain, 1946; attended the University of Wisconsin Law School and received his degree in 1949; married Nancy Barnes; practiced law in Madison, Wisconsin, in the firm of MacDonald and MacDonald, 1949–1950; became a member of the faculty of the University of Wisconsin Law School, 1950–1951; joined the legal department and moved up through the corporate structure of the Sentry Insurance Company of Stevens Point, Wisconsin, 1951–1969; served as Assistant Secretary of Defense for Administration, 30 January 1969–30 June 1971; was assigned responsibility for all Department of Defense intelligence resources and was chairman of the Defense Investigative Review Council; served as Secretary of the Army, 1 July 1971–4 May 1973; under his direction the remaining Army troops were redeployed from Vietnam, recruiting was converted to an all-volunteer basis, the administration of the Ryukyu Islands was terminated, the Civil Defense administrative role was relinquished, and Army biological warfare facilities were closed in conformance with international agreements; resigned in 1973 to resume his association with the Sentry Corporation, 1973–1979, as president; was president of the Health Insurance Association of America, 1975–1980; was president of the American Council of Life Insurance, 1980–1982; was chairman of the Equitable Life Assurance Society of the United States, 1982–1987; became president and chief executive officer of the IDS Mutual Fund Group in 1987.

The Artist

Everett Raymond Kinstler (1926–   ) studied at the Art Students League in New York and spent the first dozen years of his career as an illustrator before turning to portraiture in 1955. His portraits of public officials, both civil and military, hang in several government departments in the nation's capital, and he painted the official portrait of President Gerald R. Ford. A member of a number of art societies and a recipient of several awards, he is the author of *Painting Portraits* (1971) and illustrator of several other books. He maintains a studio in New York City.

ROBERT FREDERICK FROEHLKE
Nixon Administration

By Everett Raymond Kinstler
Oil on canvas, 39½″ x 33½″, 1973

HOWARD HOLLIS CALLAWAY was born in LaGrange, Georgia, on 2 April 1927; attended the local schools and Episcopal High School in Alexandria, Virginia; attended Georgia Institute of Technology, Atlanta, 1944–1945; graduated from the United States Military Academy, West Point, New York, 1949; married Elizabeth Walton, 1949; was commissioned a second lieutenant and served in Infantry, 1949–1952; was a platoon leader in the 17th Infantry Regiment, 7th Division, in Korea, 1949–1950; was an instructor at the Infantry School, Fort Benning, Georgia, 1951–1952; was president of Callaway Gardens, a tourist resort in Georgia, 1953–1970, and the Ida Cason Callaway Foundation, 1956–1970; served in the U.S. House of Representatives, 1965–1967; was an unsuccessful candidate for governor of Georgia, 1966; was chairman of the council of trustees of Freedoms Foundation, Valley Forge; served on the Republican National Committee; was president of Interfinancial, Incorporated, 1972; served as Secretary of the Army, 15 May 1973–3 July 1975; under his direction the phaseout of the draft was completed, the command and staff structure was reorganized, the Army served as executive agent for U.S. participation in the United Nations Truce Supervision Organization in the Middle East, and the Army celebrated its bicentennial; resigned to become manager of President Ford's campaign for election in 1976; returned to private business interests in the recreational resort field; became president of Crested Butte Resort, Colorado.

The Artist

George Augusta (1922–   ), the Boston youth who became interested in art during World War II service in Italy and went on to study there and in his native city, has painted the portraits of a number of government department heads. In addition to three Secretaries of the Army—Vance, Resor, and Callaway—he has painted the portraits of former Secretary of Defense Clark Clifford and former Secretary of Agriculture Clifford Hardin.

HOWARD HOLLIS CALLAWAY
Nixon and Ford Administrations

By George Augusta
Oil on canvas, 39½″ x 31¾″, 1975

MARTIN RICHARD HOFFMANN was born in Stockbridge, Massachusetts, on 20 April 1932; graduated from Princeton University, 1954; enlisted in the U.S. Army, 1954; was commissioned from Field Artillery Officer Candidate School, 1955; served with the 187th Regimental Combat Team and the 101st Airborne Division, 1955–1956; continued military service in the Army Reserve; married Margaret Ann McCabe; graduated from the University of Virginia Law School, 1961; served as law clerk for Judge Albert V. Bryan, U.S. Court of Appeals, Fourth Circuit, Alexandria, Virginia, 1961–1962; was assistant U.S. attorney, Washington, D.C., 1962–1965; was minority counsel, House Judiciary Committee, 1965–1966; served as legal counsel to Senator Charles H. Percy of Illinois, 1967–1969; was assistant general counsel and assistant secretary of University Computing Company, 1969–1971; was general counsel, Atomic Energy Commission, 1971–1973; was special assistant to the Secretary of Defense, 1973–1974; was general counsel of the Department of Defense, 1974–1975; served as Secretary of the Army, 5 August 1975–13 February 1977; under his direction the Army addressed the pervasive problems of post–Vietnam War readjustment, established a Privacy Review Board to act upon requests for access to records prompted by the Freedom of Information Act, and converted its operations to a new fiscal year basis; entered the private practice of law with the firm of Gardner, Carton & Douglas, 1977; became vice president and general counsel of Digital Equipment Corporation, 1989; is a member of the board of E-Systems, Inc.; is a trustee of the Association of the United States Army; served on the Secretary of Defense's Commission on Base Realignment and Closure.

The Artist

Daniel Eugene Greene (1934–   ) was born in Cincinnati, Ohio, studied at the Art Academy there, then moved to New York City to study with Robert Brackman at the Art Students League and with Robert Philipp at the National Academy. A National Academician, he has won numerous awards during the last two decades, and his works are in the collections of public and private institutions and individuals around the country. His subjects include Mrs. Eleanor Roosevelt, Governors Herbert Lehman and George Romney, Senators George Aiken and Spessard Holland, former Israeli Prime Minister David Ben Gurion, and Astronaut Walter Schirra.

MARTIN RICHARD HOFFMANN
Ford Administration

By Daniel Eugene Greene
Oil on canvas, 43″ x 35″, 1977

CLIFFORD LEOPOLD ALEXANDER, JR., was born in New York City on 21 September 1933; attended the Ethical Culture and Fieldston Schools there; graduated from Harvard University, 1955; graduated from Yale University Law School, 1958; enlisted in the New York National Guard, 1958; served briefly with the 369th Field Artillery Battalion at Fort Dix, New Jersey; married Adele Logan, 1959; was admitted to the bar; served as an assistant district attorney for New York County, 1959–1961; became executive director of the Manhattanville Hamilton Grange Neighborhood Conservation Project, then program and executive director of Harlem Youth Opportunities; practiced law in New York City; was called to Washington to serve as a foreign affairs officer on the National Security Council staff, 1963; was successively deputy special assistant to the President, associate special counsel, and deputy special counsel on the White House staff, 1964–1967; was chairman of the U.S. Equal Employment Opportunity Commission, 1967–1969; was a special representative of the President and headed the U.S. delegation to ceremonies marking the independence of the Kingdom of Swaziland, 1968; practiced law with the Washington firm of Arnold and Porter, 1969–1975; was a television news commentator in Washington, 1972–1976; was a professor of law at Howard University, 1973–1974; ran unsuccessfully as a candidate for mayor of the District of Columbia, 1974; became a partner in the law firm of Verner, Liipfert, Bernhard, McPherson, and Alexander, 1975; served as Secretary of the Army, 14 February 1977–20 January 1981; concentrated upon making the all-volunteer Army work, stressed programs to enhance professionalism, and emphasized the award of contracts to minority businesses; formed the consulting firm of Alexander and Associates, 1981; serves on the boards of directors of several national corporations; is a member of the Board of Governors of the American Stock Exchange.

The Artist

Harrison Edward Benton, Jr., has been an artist for as long as he can remember. He received his Bachelor of Fine Arts degree from Maryland Institute of Art, Baltimore, Maryland. His entire career has been oriented toward art. A longtime Department of Defense employee, he currently heads Presentations and Graphics in the Directorate of Programs and Evaluation for the U.S. Air Force. In recognition of his accomplishments as a portrait artist, he has been inducted into the prestigious Society of Illustrators (New York) and the American Portrait Society.

CLIFFORD LEOPOLD ALEXANDER, JR.
Carter Administration

By Harrison Edward Benton, Jr.
Oil on canvas, 53" x 41", 1984

JOHN OTHO MARSH, JR., was born in Winchester, Virginia, on 7 August 1926; attended the public schools at Harrisonburg, Virginia; entered the U.S. Army in 1944, was commissioned through the Officer Candidate Course at the Infantry School, 1945, and served with the occupation forces in Germany, 1945–1947; was a member of the United States Army Reserve, 1947–1951; married Glenn Ann Patterson, 1950; graduated from Washington and Lee University, 1951, was admitted to the Virginia bar, 1952, and entered the practice of law in Strasburg, Virginia; was town judge of Strasburg and town attorney of New Market, Virginia, 1954–1962; served four terms in the U.S. House of Representatives from Virginia's Seventh District, 1963–1971; resumed the practice of law in Washington, D.C.; entered service in the Army National Guard in Virginia in 1951, graduating from the Army's Airborne Infantry School with a senior parachutist rating in 1964 and retiring from Guard service as a lieutenant colonel in 1976; was a member of the American Revolution Bicentennial Commission, 1966–1970; was Assistant Secretary of Defense for Legislative Affairs, 1973–1974; was a counselor to President Gerald R. Ford, 1974–1977; resumed the practice of law with the firm of Mays, Valentine, Davenport, and Moore; is a member of the Board of Visitors of the Virginia Military Institute; served as Secretary of the Army, 30 January 1981–14 August 1989, holding the office longer than any previous Secretary; during his tenure the Army observed the Bicentennial of the founding of the country, implemented the provisions of the Goldwater-Nichols Act making the services more oriented to joint operations, and reorganized the Army Staff to eliminate duplication of functions; is chairman, Reserve Forces Policy Board.

The Artist

Sylvia Rogers Barnes has been a professional artist for eighteen years. She has received numerous awards from the Society of Western Artists, has been a staff painter with Faces West Art Gallery and Studio, and is one of California's important portrait painters. For four years she taught art at the Mt. Diablo School District, and since 1980 she has been a free-lance artist in the Monterey-Carmel area.

JOHN OTHO MARSH, JR.
Reagan-Bush Administrations

By Sylvia Rogers Barnes
Oil on canvas, 42" x 35", 1990

MICHAEL PATRICK WILLIAM STONE, the only foreign-born Secretary of the Army, was born in London, England, on 2 June 1925; has resided in the United States since 1929; served with the British Royal Navy, 1943–1945, received pilot training in the United States, and served in the Mediterranean and Far East as a member of the Royal Naval Air Squadron 1831, which completed its World War II service by participating in the surrender of the Japanese forces at Rabaul, New Guinea, in September 1945; graduated from Yale University in 1948; studied law at New York University Law School; married Ann Donogh, 1952; was a founding partner of Sterling International, a paper marketing and manufacturing company in San Francisco in the early 1950's; was vice president of that company and president of several of its subsidiaries including Sterling Vineyards, 1960–1982; was the Director of the U.S. Mission for the Agency for International Development (AID) in Cairo, Egypt, 1982–1985; was involved in implementing the Kissinger Commission recommendations in the Caribbean Basin Initiative countries, 1985–1986; was Assistant Secretary of the Army for Financial Management, 1986–1988, and cochaired the Army's Commission to Implement the Defense Reorganization Act of 1986 (Goldwater-Nichols), resulting in the most sweeping changes to the Army in years; served concurrently as the Acting Under Secretary of the Army from 28 February to 23 May 1988; was Under Secretary of the Army and Army Acquisition Executive, 1988–1989; simultaneously performed the duties of the Under Secretary of Defense for Acquisition from 13 May 1989 until 10 August 1989; was sworn in as the fifteenth Secretary of the Army on 14 August 1989; under his direction the Army participated in Operations JUST CAUSE (Panama) and DESERT SHIELD and DESERT STORM (Southwest Asia); during his tenure the Cold War victory was finally achieved and the Army reshaped itself for the post–Cold War era.

The Artist

John Boyd Martin (1936–   ) graduated from the University of Kansas School of Fine Arts and began his career as an advertising art director and illustrator, winning more than 150 awards for his work before turning to portraiture. Commissioned by major universities, professional sports franchises, business institutions, and private collections, his portraits include golfers Arnold Palmer and Jack Nicklaus; the former CEO of General Dynamics, David Lewis; the former Director of the FAA, Allan McArtor; and the President of Trinity University, Dr. Ronald Calgaard.

MICHAEL PATRICK WILLIAM STONE
Bush Administration

By John Boyd Martin
Oil on canvas, 42" x 35", 1992

Appendixes
Bibliographies

APPENDIX A

SECRETARIES OF WAR AD INTERIM
AND
ACTING SECRETARIES OF THE ARMY

Change is the rule rather than the exception in the political process, and the constant rotation of officials at the upper levels of government causes frequent gaps in executive progression. Interruptions may result from a change of administration or through the dismissal, reassignment, resignation, illness, or death of an incumbent. Although continuity is normally maintained by second-level management, intervals are usually bridged by temporary executive appointees. The Army department has had its share of secretaries ad interim over the years.

Acting secretaries have come from the civilian and military ranks of the department and from other agencies of government, and tours have ranged from a few days to as long as one year. When Secretary Pickering was commissioned Secretary of State by President Washington on 10 December 1795, he retained the Army portfolio as well and served until Secretary McHenry took office on 27 January 1796. Under similar circumstances, Secretary Dexter retained the Army stewardship after being appointed Secretary of the Treasury by President John Adams on 31 January 1801, until Secretary Dearborn succeeded him at the War Department on 5 March 1801. The roles were reversed when President Madison asked Secretary of the Treasury Alexander J. Dallas to relieve ailing Secretary Monroe of the Army responsibility so that Monroe could devote full time to his primary duties as Secretary of State. Dallas filled in at the War Department from 2 March to 1 August 1815.

On 22 October 1816, effective with Secretary William H. Crawford's transfer from the War Department to the Treasury Department, George Graham, Chief Clerk of the War Department, was designated Acting Secretary by President Madison under special Congressional authority, and held the position for almost a year until Secretary Calhoun's arrival on 8 October 1817. Again, in a six-week hiatus between the departure of Secretary Eaton on 18 June 1831 and the assumption of office by Secretary Cass on 1 August 1831, Secretary of the Navy Levi Woodbury served concurrently as Secretary of War.

Following Cass's five-year superintendence, Attorney General Benjamin F. Butler was designated by President Jackson to preside over the War Department as well, a commission that extended from Secretary Cass's departure on 5 October 1836 until Secretary Poinsett's appointment on 7 March 1837 in the opening week of President Van Buren's administration.

Another interval occurred in the succeeding Tyler administration between the tours of Secretaries Bell and Spencer. Once again it was the War Department's Chief Clerk who supervised operations; Albert Miller Lea watched over the department from 13 September to 12 October 1841.

On several occasions in the nineteenth century and one in the twentieth, the executive branch of government strayed briefly from the path of civilian control over the military when the President designated the Army's senior uniformed official to act temporarily as Secretary of War. President Fillmore, for example, during his first days in office, designated Lieutenant General Winfield Scott, the Commanding General of the Army, to act as Secretary of War during the interregnum between the departure of Secretary George W. Crawford on 23 July 1850 and the succession by Secretary Conrad on 15 August 1850.

Three interruptions in the secretarial progression occurred during the 1860's: one was covered by another cabinet officer, the other two by military officers. In the first, President Buchanan asked Postmaster General Joseph Holt to also oversee the War Department after Secretary Floyd departed on 29 December 1860. Holt filled the post on an acting basis until 18 January 1861, when the President appointed him Secretary of War; confirmed by the Congress, Holt continued in office until President Lincoln's inauguration in March.

When relations between President Lincoln's Secretary of War, Edwin M. Stanton, and Lincoln's successor, President Andrew Johnson, soured, the Chief Executive suspended Stanton on 12 August 1867 and appointed General Ulysses S. Grant, Commanding General of the Army, as Secretary of War ad interim. Although ill-disposed to be at the center of a controversy between his departmental superior and his commander in chief, Grant acted as secretary until 13 January 1868, when the Senate reinstated Stanton. Grant managed to hold himself apart from the political turmoil which led to unsuccessful impeachment proceedings against President Johnson and Stanton's early resignation.

As Johnson's successor, President Grant also turned to the Commanding General of the Army to fill the secretarial post temporarily when Secretary Rawlin's health failed. General William T. Sherman ran the department from 6 September to 25

October 1869, when Secretary Belknap entered office.

The final secretarial interregnum of the nineteenth century came late in 1891 during President Benjamin Harrison's administration. Upon Secretary Proctor's departure from office on 5 November 1891, Assistant Secretary of War Lewis A. Grant became Acting Secretary for a period of six weeks until Secretary Elkins entered office on 17 December 1891.

The creation of the posts of Assistant Secretary of War in 1861 and Under Secretary of War in 1940—both titles carried forward with the department's 1947 name change from War to Army—provided a pool of resident officials who were intimately informed concerning departmental affairs and were ready to serve in an acting capacity should the need arise. The one exception in the twentieth century occurred when Maj. Gen. Hugh L. Scott officiated as Secretary of War at President Wilson's request following the simultaneous departures of Secretary Garrison and Assistant Secretary Breckinridge on 10 February 1916 and until Secretary Baker's arrival on 9 March 1916. Otherwise, during the current century, interim officials have been drawn from the second-level civilian officials of the department.

On 18 November 1929, for example, Assistant Secretary of War Patrick J. Hurley became Acting Secretary upon the death of incumbent Secretary Good. Nominated to succeed Mr. Good, Hurley became Secretary of War in his own right on 9 December 1929. Under similar circumstances, Assistant Secretary Harry H. Woodring assumed the secretaryship on an acting basis when Secretary Dern died in office on 27 August 1936, moving of-ficially into the executive role a month later, on 25 September 1936. Woodring resigned on 20 June 1940, and Assistant Secretary Louis A. Johnson ran the department in an acting capacity until Secretary Stimson entered office on 10 July 1940.

There have been several interruptions in secretarial continuity since the 1947 change in departmental designation and the loss of cabinet status which resulted from the 1949 amendments to the National Security Act. Gordon Gray, who was an Assistant Secretary of the Army under Secretary Royall and advanced to Under Secretary after Royall's departure, was Acting Secretary from 28 April to 19 June 1949 before moving up the final step to become Secretary of the Army. Again, from 20 January to 4 February 1953, Under Secretary Earl D. Johnson acted as Secretary of the Army, bridging the departure of Secretary Pace and the arrival of Secretary Stevens. Only a few days separated the incumbencies of Secretaries Brucker and Stahr, Stahr and Vance, and Ailes and Resor, and other transitions were made by immediate succession; the next substantial interval came between the departure of Secretary Callaway on 3 July 1975 and the arrival of Secretary Hoffmann on 5 August, a period in which Under Secretary Norman R. Augustine was Acting Secretary of the Army

The War Department commissioned the portraits of seven interim secretaries. The gallery contains paintings of Alexander J. Dallas by Philip F. Wharton; Benjamin F. Butler by Robert Walter Weir; Reverdy Johnson (who served a five-day interval) by Henry Ulke; Winfield Scott by Weir; Ulysses S. Grant by Freeman Thorp; William T. Sherman by George P. A. Healy; and Hugh L. Scott by Edmund C. Tarbell.

Secretaries Ad Interim

Name		Dates	
Alexander J. Dallas	2 March	1815– 1 August	1815
George Graham	22 October	1816– 8 October	1817
Levi Woodbury	18 June	1831– 1 August	1831
Benjamin F. Butler	5 October	1836– 7 March	1837
Albert Miller Lea	13 September	1841–12 October	1841
Winfield Scott	23 July	1850–15 August	1850
Joseph Holt	29 December	1860–18 January	1861
Ulysses S. Grant	12 August	1867–13 January	1868
William T. Sherman	6 September	1869–25 October	1869
Lewis A. Grant	5 November	1891–17 December	1891
Hugh L. Scott	10 February	1916– 9 March	1916
Patrick J. Hurley	18 November	1929– 9 December	1929
Harry H. Woodring	27 August	1936–25 September	1936
Louis A. Johnson	20 June	1940–10 July	1940
Gordon Gray	28 April	1949–19 June	1949
Earl D. Johnson	20 January	1953– 4 February	1953
Norman R. Augustine	3 July	1975– 5 August	1975

APPENDIX B

CHRONOLOGICAL LIST OF PRESIDENTS OF THE UNITED STATES, SECRETARIES OF WAR, AND SECRETARIES OF THE ARMY

President [1]	Secretary of War	
George Washington 30 Apr 1789– 3 Mar 1797	Henry Knox	12 Sep 1789–31 Dec 1794
	Timothy Pickering	2 Jan 1795–10 Dec 1795
	James McHenry	27 Jan 1796–
John Quincy Adams 4 Mar 1797– 3 Mar 1801	James McHenry	–13 May 1800
	Samuel Dexter	13 May 1800–31 Jan 1801
Thomas Jefferson 4 Mar 1801– 3 Mar 1809	Henry Dearborn	5 Mar 1801–
James Madison 4 Mar 1809– 3 Mar 1817	Henry Dearborn	– 7 Mar 1809
	William Eustis	7 Mar 1809–13 Jan 1813
	John Armstrong	13 Jan 1813–27 Sep 1814
	James Monroe	27 Sep 1814– 2 Mar 1815
	William H. Crawford	1 Aug 1815–22 Oct 1816
James Monroe 4 Mar 1817– 3 Mar 1825	John C. Calhoun	8 Oct 1817–
John Quincy Adams 4 Mar 1825– 3 Mar 1829	John C. Calhoun	– 7 Mar 1825
	James Barbour	7 Mar 1825–23 May 1828
	Peter B. Porter	26 May 1828–

[1] The question of whether the President's term of office expired at midnight of 3 March or noon of 4 March was not spelled out in the United States Constitution and became the subject of a variety of interpretations in the early years of the republic. In 1821, Secretary of State John Quincy Adams, apparently at President Monroe's request, asked Chief Justice John Marshall for an expression on the subject. The Chief Justice, noting that he had "conversed with my brethren on the subject," stated that "As the constitution only provides that the President shall take the oath it 'prescribes before he enter on the execution of his office,' and as the law is silent on the subject, the time seems to be in some measure at the discretion of that high officer. There is an obvious propriety in taking the oath as soon as it can conveniently be taken, & thereby shortening the interval in which the executive power is suspended. But some interval is inevitable. The time of the actual President will expire, and that of the President elect commence, at twelve in the night of the 3d of March. It has been usual to take the oath at mid day on the 4th...." On the basis of this statement, somewhat in the nature of an advisory opinion of the Supreme Court, the date of 3 March is used in this chart as the limit of the incumbent's term of office, and 4 March as the start of the successor's term. The question was finally resolved in law in 1933 with the ratification of the Twentieth Amendment to the Constitution, which changed the inaugural date to 20 January and set noon as the hour for the presidential transition.

APPENDIX B—Continued

President	Secretary of War	
Andrew Jackson 4 Mar 1829– 3 Mar 1837	Peter B. Porter	– 9 Mar 1829
	John H. Eaton	9 Mar 1829–18 Jun 1831
	Lewis Cass	1 Aug1831– 5 Oct 1836
Martin Van Buren 4 Mar 1837– 3 Mar 1841	Joel R. Poinsett	7 Mar 1837–
William Henry Harrison 4 Mar 1841– 4 Apr 1841	Joel R. Poinsett	– 5 Mar 1841
	John Bell	5 Mar 1841–
John Tyler 6 Apr 1841– 3 Mar 1845	John Bell	–13 Sep 1841
	John C. Spencer	12 Oct 1841– 3 Mar 1843
	James M. Porter	8 Mar 1843–30 Jan 1844
	William Wilkins	15 Feb 1844– 4 Mar 1845
James K. Polk 4 Mar 1845– 3 Mar 1849	William L. Marcy	6 Mar 1845– 5 Mar 1849
Zachary Taylor 5 Mar 1849– 9 Jul 1850	George W. Crawford	8 Mar 1849–
Millard Fillmore 10 Jul 1850– 3 Mar 1853	George W. Crawford	–23 Jul 1850
	Charles M. Conrad	15 Aug 1850–
Franklin Pierce 4 Mar 1853– 3 Mar 1857	Charles M. Conrad	– 7 Mar 1853
	Jefferson Davis	7 Mar 1853–
James Buchanan 4 Mar 1857– 3 Mar 1861	Jefferson Davis	– 6 Mar 1857
	John B. Floyd	6 Mar 1857–29 Dec 1860
	Joseph Holt	18 Jan 1861–
Abraham Lincoln 4 Mar 1861– 15 Apr 1865	Joseph Holt	– 5 Mar 1861
	Simon Cameron	5 Mar 1861–15 Jan 1862
	Edwin M. Stanton	20 Jan 1862–
Andrew Johnson 15 Apr 1865– 3 Mar 1869	Edwin M. Stanton	–28 May 1868
	John M. Schofield	1 Jun 1868–

APPENDIX B—Continued

President	Secretary of War	
Ulysses S. Grant 4 Mar 1869– 3 Mar 1877	John M. Schofield	–13 Mar 1869
	John A. Rawlins	13 Mar 1869– 6 Sep 1869
	William W. Belknap	25 Oct 1869– 2 Mar 1876
	Alphonso Taft	8 Mar 1876–22 May 1876
	James D. Cameron	22 May 1876– 3 Mar 1877
Rutherford B. Hayes 4 Mar 1877– 3 Mar 1881	George W. McCrary	12 Mar 1877–10 Dec 1879
	Alexander Ramsey	10 Dec 1879–
James A. Garfield 4 Mar 1881–19 Sep 1881	Alexander Ramsey	– 5 Mar 1881
	Robert T. Lincoln	5 Mar 1881–
Chester A. Arthur 20 Sep 1881– 3 Mar 1885	Robert T. Lincoln	–
Grover Cleveland 4 Mar 1885– 3 Mar 1889	Robert T. Lincoln	– 5 Mar 1885
	William C. Endicott	5 Mar 1885–
Benjamin Harrison 4 Mar 1889– 3 Mar 1893	William C. Endicott	– 5 Mar 1889
	Redfield Proctor	5 Mar 1889– 5 Nov 1891
	Stephen B. Elkins	17 Dec 1891–
Grover Cleveland 4 Mar 1893– 3 Mar 1897	Stephen B. Elkins	– 5 Mar 1893
	Daniel S. Lamont	5 Mar 1893–
William McKinley 4 Mar 1897–14 Sep 1901	Daniel S. Lamont	– 5 Mar 1897
	Russell A. Alger	5 Mar 1897– 1 Aug 1899
	Elihu Root	1 Aug 1899–
Theodore Roosevelt 14 Sep 1901– 3 Mar 1909	Elihu Root	–31 Jan 1904
	William H. Taft	1 Feb 1904–30 Jun 1908
	Luke E. Wright	1 Jul 1908–
William H. Taft 4 Mar 1909– 3 Mar 1913	Luke E. Wright	–11 Mar 1909
	Jacob M. Dickinson	12 Mar 1909–21 May 1911
	Henry L. Stimson	22 May 1911– 4 Mar 1913
Woodrow Wilson 4 Mar 1913– 3 Mar 1921	Lindley M. Garrison	5 Mar 1913–10 Feb 1916
	Newton D. Baker	9 Mar 1916– 4 Mar 1921
Warren G. Harding 4 Mar 1921– 2 Aug 1923	John W. Weeks	5 Mar 1921–

APPENDIX B—Continued

President	Secretary of War	
Calvin Coolidge 3 Aug 1923– 3 Mar 1929	John W. Weeks	–13 Oct 1925
	Dwight F. Davis .... 14 Oct	1925–
Herbert C. Hoover 4 Mar 1929– 3 Mar 1933	Dwight F. Davis	– 5 Mar 1929
	James W. Good .... 6 Mar	1929–18 Nov 1929
	Patrick J. Hurley .... 9 Dec	1929– 3 Mar 1933
Franklin D. Roosevelt 4 Mar 1933–12 Apr 1945	George H. Dern .... 4 Mar	1933–27 Aug 1936
	Harry H. Woodring .... 25 Sep	1936–20 Jun 1940
	Henry L. Stimson .... 10 Jul	1940–
Harry S. Truman 12 Apr 1945–20 Jan 1953	Henry L. Stimson	–21 Sep 1945
	Robert P. Patterson .... 27 Sep	1945–18 Jul 1947
	Kenneth C. Royall .... 19 Jul	1947–17 Sep 1947

Secretary of the Army

President	Secretary of the Army	
	Kenneth C. Royall .... 17 Sep	1947–27 Apr 1949
	Gordon Gray .... 20 Jun	1949–12 Apr 1950
	Frank Pace, Jr. .... 12 Apr	1950–20 Jan 1953
Dwight D. Eisenhower 20 Jan 1953–20 Jan 1961	Robert T. Stevens .... 4 Feb	1953–21 Jul 1955
	Wilber M. Brucker .... 21 Jul	1955–19 Jan 1961
John F. Kennedy 20 Jan 1961–22 Nov 1963	Elvis J. Stahr, Jr. .... 25 Jan	1961–30 Jun 1962
	Cyrus R. Vance .... 5 Jul	1962–
Lyndon B. Johnson 22 Nov 1963–20 Jan 1969	Cyrus R. Vance	–21 Jan 1964
	Stephen Ailes .... 28 Jan	1964– 1 Jul 1965
	Stanley R. Resor .... 2 Jul	1965–
Richard M. Nixon 20 Jan 1969– 9 Aug 1974	Stanley R. Resor	–20 Jun 1971
	Robert F. Froehlke .... 1 Jul	1971–14 May 1973
	Howard H. Callaway .... 15 May	1973–
Gerald R. Ford 9 Aug 1974–20 Jan 1977	Howard H. Callaway	–3 Jul 1975
	Martin R. Hoffmann .... 5 Aug	1975–
James E. Carter 20 Jan 1977–20 Jan 1981	Martin R. Hoffmann	–13 Feb 1977
	Clifford L. Alexander, Jr. .... 14 Feb	1977–20 Jan 1981
Ronald W. Reagan 20 Jan 1981–20 Jan 1989	John O. Marsh, Jr. .... 29 Jan	1981–14 Aug 1989
George Bush 20 Jan 1989–	Michael P. W. Stone .... 14 Aug	1989–

GENERAL BIBLIOGRAPHY

The literature of an institution and its leaders over an extended period of time is bound to be uneven. The Army's history during two hundred years of American statehood has moved with national currents, and the administrations of its civilian heads have taken historical form from the fluctuation in the events of their times and the nature of the individuals' participation in those events. Add to this the disparities in individual abilities and terms of office, as well as the fact that some officials had wider and more influential public service than others, and it is readily apparent that there will be marked differences in the degree of biographical attention accorded to Army secretaries over the period from 1776, when the Board of War was established, up to the present.

It is also understandable that earlier figures who served a young and growing nation in a smaller and more focused government should come under closer scrutiny from the perspective of time. Additionally,

no Secretary of War is still living, and public figures are more easily and freely assessed after they have left the scene than while they are still living. In light of the office's loss of cabinet status and the subordination of the service departments within the Department of Defense, it remains to be seen whether the Army secretarial office and the incumbents of modern times will garner the attention accorded their predecessors in the more sovereign and independent War Department days.

It was deemed most useful to the reader to divide the select bibliography into two sections: a general source list pertaining to military history and a specific one dealing with the individual secretaries (including the officials who served ad interim) and the artists who painted them. The bibliography that follows immediately includes works on the national defense, the history of the Army, the departmental headquarters, and the broad details of organization and operation.

American State Papers: Military Affairs. 7 vols. Washington: Gales and Seaton, 1832–1861.

Annual Reports of the Secretary of War, 1822–1949. Washington: Government Printing Office.

Annual Reports of the Secretary of the Army, 1950–1968. In *Annual Report of the Department of Defense.* Washington: Government Printing Office.

Ball, Harry P. *Of Responsible Command: A History of the U.S. Army War College.* Carlisle: Alumni Association U.S. Army War College, 1984.

Berdahl, Clarence. *War Powers of the Executive of the United States.* Urbana: University of Illinois Press, 1921.

Bernardo, C. Joseph, and Bacon, Eugene H. *American Military Policy: Its Development Since 1775.* Harrisburg: Stackpole, 1955.

Borklund, Carl. *Men of the Pentagon: From Forrestal to McNamara.* New York: Frederick A. Praeger, 1966.

———. *The Department of Defense.* New York: Frederick A. Praeger, 1968.

Clark, Keith C., and Legere, Laurence J. *The President and the Management of National Security.* New York: Frederick A. Praeger, 1969.

Coffman, Edward M. *The Old Army: A Portrait of the American Army in Peacetime.* New York: Cambridge University Press, 1988.

Curti, Merle. *Peace or War: The American Struggle, 1636–1936.* New York: W. W. Norton, 1936.

Department of the Army Historical Summary. Washington: Government Printing Office, 1970–86.

Dupuy, R. Ernest. *The Compact History of the United States Army.* New York: Hawthorn, 1956.

———, and Dupuy, Trevor N. *Military Heritage of America.* New York: McGraw-Hill Book Co., 1956.

Eberstadt, Ferdinand. *Unification of War and Navy Departments and Postwar Organization for National Security. A Report to Hon. James Forrestal.* Washington: Government Printing Office, 1945.

Ekirch, Arthur A., Jr. *The Civilian and the Military.* New York: Oxford University Press, 1956.

Ganoe, William Addleman. *The History of the United States Army.* New York: D. Appleton & Co., 1924.

Hammond, Paul Y. *Organizing for Defense: The American Military Establishment in the Twentieth Century.* Princeton: Princeton University Press, 1961.

Heitman, Francis B. *Historical Register and Dictionary of the United States Army.* Washington: Government Printing Office, 1903.

Hewes, James E., Jr. *From Root to McNamara: Army Organization and Administration, 1900–1963.* Washington: Government Printing Office, 1975.

Hill, Jim Dan. *The Minute Man in Peace and War: A History of the National Guard.* Harrisburg: Stackpole, 1964.

Huntington, Samuel P. *The Soldier and the State: The Theory and Politics of Civil-Military Relations.* Cambridge: Harvard University Press, 1957.

Ingersoll, Lurton D. *A History of the War Department of the United States with Biographical Sketches of the Secretaries.* Washington: Francis B. Mohun, 1880.

Jacobs, James Ripley. *The Beginning of the U.S. Army, 1783–1812.* Princeton: Princeton University Press, 1947.

Kauffman, William W., ed. *Military Policy and National Security.* Princeton: Princeton University Press, 1956.

Kerwin, Jerome G., ed. *Civil-Military Relationship in American Life.* Chicago: University of Chicago Press, 1948.

Kohn, Richard H. *Eagle and Sword: The Federalists and the Creation of the Military Establishment in America, 1783–1802.* New York: Free Press, 1975.

Kreidberg, Marvin A., and Henry, Merton G. *History of Military Mobilization in the United States Army, 1775–1945.* Washington: Government Printing Office, 1984.

Mahon, John K. *History of the Militia and the National Guard.* New York: Macmillan Co., 1983.

Matloff, Maurice, ed. *American Military History.* Washington: Government Printing Office, 1969. Revised edition, 1989.

May, Ernest R., ed. *The Ultimate Decision: The President as Commander in Chief.* New York: George Braziller, 1960.

Meneely, Alexander H. *The War Department, 1861: A Study in Mobilization and Administration.* New York: Columbia University Press, 1928.

Millis, Walter. *Arms and Men: A Study in American Military History.* New York: G. P. Putnam's Sons, 1956.

———, with Mansfield, Harvey C., and Stein, Harold. *Arms and the State: Civil-Military Elements in National Policy.* New York: Twentieth Century Fund, 1958.

Nelson, Otto L. *National Security and the General Staff.* Washington: Infantry Journal Press, 1946.

Palmer, John McAuley. *America in Arms: The Experience of the United States with Military Organization.* New Haven: Yale University Press, 1941.

Powers, Patrick W. *A Guide to National Defense: The Organization and Operations of the U.S. Military Establishment.* New York: Frederick A. Praeger, 1964.

Prucha, Francis P. *The Sword of the Republic: The United States Army on the Frontier.* Lincoln: University of Nebraska Press, 1986.

Ries, John C. *The Management of Defense: Organization and Control of the U.S. Armed Forces.* Baltimore: Johns Hopkins University Press, 1964.

Rodenbough, Theophilus F., and Haskin, William L., eds. *The Army of the United States: Historical Sketches of Staff and Line.* New York: Merrill, 1896.

Sanders, Jennings B. *The Evolution of the Executive Department, 1774–1789.* Chapel Hill: University of North Carolina Press, 1935.

Smith, Louis. *American Democracy and Military Power: A Study of Civil Control of the Military Power in the United States.* Chicago: University of Chicago Press, 1951.

Spaulding, Oliver Lyman. *The United States Army in War and Peace.* New York: G. P. Putnam's Sons, 1937.

Stanley, Timothy W. *American Defense and National Security.* Washington: Public Affairs Press, 1956.

Thian, Raphael P. *Legislative History of the General Staff of the Army of the United States.* Washington: Government Printing Office, 1901.

Upton, Emory. *The Military Policy of the United States from 1775.* Washington: Government Printing Office, 1904.

Ward, Harry M. *The Department of War, 1781–1795.* Pittsburgh: University of Pittsburgh Press, 1962.

Weigley, Russell F. *History of the United States Army.* New York: Macmillan Co., 1967. Enlarged edition, Bloomington: University of Indiana Press, 1984.

———. *The American Way of War.* New York: Macmillan Co., 1973.

———. *Towards an American Army: Military Thought from Washington to Marshall.* New York: Columbia University Press, 1962.

White, Howard. *Executive Influence in Determining Military Policy in the United States.* Urbana: University of Illinois Press, 1924.

Williams, T. Harry. *Americans at War: The Development of the American Military System.* Baton Rouge: Louisiana State University Press, 1956.

Wright, Robert K., Jr. *The Continental Army.* Washington: Government Printing Office, 1983.

Yoshpe, Harry B., and Falk, Stanley L. *Organization for National Security.* Washington: Industrial College of the Armed Forces, 1963.

BIBLIOGRAPHY
OF
SECRETARIES AND ARTISTS

Most of the Secretaries of War and Secretaries of the Army have received brief biographical mention in standard reference works. Principal among these, insofar as the earlier officials are concerned, is the twenty-volume *Dictionary of American Biography,* with supplements, and the thirty-two volume *National Cyclopaedia of American Biography.* Eight secretaries are treated in the four-volume *The National Portrait Gallery of Distinguished Americans* (1834–1839). The various editions of *Who's Who in America* and *Who Was Who in America* contain references to individuals—especially later officials—who may have had little or no biographical treatment in other sources. *Current Biography* is also useful for its coverage of contemporary officials. Treatment according to editorial perceptions of the relative importance of individuals is provided in various editions of the *Encyclopedia Americana* and *Encyclopedia Britannica* while officials of military background are also covered in Francis B. Heitman's *Historical Register and Dictionary of the United States Army* (1789–1903), George W. Cullum's *Biographical Register of the Officers and Graduates of the United States Military Academy,* a work spanning the years 1802–1950 and periodically updated, and *Who Was Who in American History— The Military.*

Autobiographies and the secondary literature on the Army's top civilian leaders provide the real substance of their lives and service. If the major published autobiographies and biographies are sup-

plemented by L. D. Ingersoll's *History of the War Department* with its biographical sketches of the first thirty-three secretaries (including those who served ad interim), and by doctoral dissertations, most of the gaps in the secretarial bibliography are filled, however imperfectly. (Doctoral dissertations are normally available in xerographic or microfilm reproduction from University Microfilms of Ann Arbor, Michigan.)

The bibliographical listing which follows includes works on the Secretaries of War and the Secretaries of the Army, the predecessors of the Secretary of War and the officials who served ad interim through the years, and the artists who painted the secretarial portraits. These are arranged alphabetically by the individual subject with applicable sources entered alphabetically under each individual's name. Since Ingersoll's *History of the War Department* includes biographical information on the first thirty-three secretaries, this source is not listed under all the individual names, but should be consulted for information on secretaries who served before 1880. Although full-length treatment is available on only a few artists, some are covered in such art reference works as George C. Groce's and David Wallace's *The New York Historical Society's Dictionary of Artists in America* and Mantle Fielding's *Dictionary of American Painters.* Several of the more prominent artists appear in the standard biographical reference works cited earlier.

Alger, Russell Alexander

Russell Alexander Alger, Late Senator in the Congress of the United States from Michigan. Lansing: n.p., 1907.

Armstrong, John

Armstrong, John. *Notices on the War of 1812.* 2 vols. New York: Wiley and Putnam, 1840.

Skeen, C. Edward. "John Armstrong and the Role of the Secretary of War in the War of 1812." Ph.D. dissertation, Ohio State University, 1966.

———. *John Armstrong, 1758–1843: A Biography.* Syracuse: Syracuse University Press, 1981.

Baker, Newton Diehl

Beaver, Daniel R. *Newton D. Baker and the American War Effort, 1917–1919.* Lincoln: University of Nebraska Press, 1966.

Cramer, C. H. *Newton D. Baker: A Biography.* Cleveland: World Publishing Co., 1961.

Palmer, Frederick. *Newton D. Baker: America at War.* 2 vols. New York: Dodd, Mead & Co., 1931.

Barbour, James

Long, William S. *James Barbour.* n.p., 1913.

Lowery, Charles D. *James Barbour: A Jeffersonian Republican.* University: University of Alabama Press, 1984.

Belknap, William Worth

Impeachment of William W. Belknap, Late Secretary of War. Washington: Government Printing Office, 1876.

Bell, John

The Life, Speeches, and Public Service of John Bell. New York: Rudd and Carleton, 1860.

Parks, Joseph H. *John Bell of Tennessee.* Baton Rouge: Louisiana State University Press, 1950.

Brucker, Wilber Marion

Brucker, Clara H. *To Have Your Cake and Eat It.* New York: Vantage Press, 1968.

Butler, Benjamin Franklin

Mallan, William D. "General Benjamin Franklin Butler." Ph.D. dissertation, University of Minnesota, 1942.

Calhoun, John Caldwell

Calhoun, John Caldwell. *Life of John C. Calhoun. Presenting a Condensed History of Political Events From 1811 to 1843.* New York: Harper & Bros., 1843.

Coit, Margaret L. *John C. Calhoun, American Portrait.* Boston: Houghton Mifflin Co., 1950.

Current, Richard N. *John C. Calhoun.* New York: Washington Square Press, 1963.

Hunt, Gaillard. *John C. Calhoun.* Philadelphia: G. W. Jacobs Co., 1908.

Jenkins, John S. *The Life of John C. Calhoun.* Rochester: Alden & Beardsley, 1856.

Meigs, William Montgomery. *The Life of John Caldwell Calhoun.* New York: G. E. Stechert & Co., 1925.

Niven, John. *John C. Calhoun and the Price of Union: A Biography.* Baton Rouge: Louisiana State University Press, 1988.

The Papers of John C. Calhoun. 20 vols. to date. Columbia: University of South Carolina Press, 1959–1991.

Thomas, John L., ed. *John C. Calhoun: A Profile.* New York: Hill & Wang, 1968.

Wiltse, Charles M. *John C. Calhoun, 1782–1828.* 3 vols. Indianapolis: Bobbs-Merrill Co., 1944–1951.

Cameron, Simon

Bradley, Erwin S. *Simon Cameron, Lincoln's Secretary of War: A Political Biography.* Philadelphia: University of Pennsylvania Press, 1966.

Cass, Lewis

Hewlett, Richard G. "Lewis Cass in National Politics, 1842–1862." Ph.D. dissertation, University of Chicago, 1952.

Hickman, George H. *The Life of General Lewis Cass.* Baltimore: N. Hickman, 1848.

McLaughlin, Andrew C. *Lewis Cass.* Boston: Houghton Mifflin Co., 1879 and 1972.

Smith, William L. *Fifty Years of Public Life: The Life and Times of Lewis Cass.* New York: Derby and Jackson, 1856.

Woodford, Frank B. *Lewis Cass: The Last Jeffersonian.* New Brunswick: Rutgers University Press, 1950.

Chandor, Douglas

Vaughn, Malcolm. *Chandor's Portraits.* New York: Brentano, 1942.

Chase, Joseph Cummings

Chase, Joseph Cummings. *My Friends Look Better Than Ever.* New York: Longmans, Green and Co., 1950.

Crawford, William Harris

Butler, Benjamin F. [Americanus]. *Sketches of the Life and Character of William H. Crawford.* Albany: Packard and Van Benthuysen, 1824.

Cutler, Everette W. *William Harris Crawford.* Charlotte: University of North Carolina Press, 1965.

Knowlton, Daniel C., ed. *The Journal of William H. Crawford.* Northhampton: Dept. of History, Smith College, 1925.

Mooney, Chase C. *William H. Crawford, 1772–1834.* Lexington: University Press of Kentucky, 1974.

Shipp, John E. D. *Giant Days, or, The Life and Times of William H. Crawford.* Americus: Southern Printers, 1909.

Dallas, Alexander James

Dallas, George M. *Life and Writings of Alexander James Dallas.* Philadelphia: J. B. Lippincott Co., 1871.

Walters, Raymond, Jr. *Alexander James Dallas: Lawyer, Politician, Financier, 1759–1817.* Philadelphia: University of Pennsylvania Press, 1943; and New York: Da Capo Press, 1969.

Davis, Jefferson

Addey, Markinfield. *Life of Jefferson Davis.* Philadelphia: Keystone Publishing Co., 1890.

Alfriend, Frank H. *The Life of Jefferson Davis.* Philadelphia: National Publishing Co., 1868.

Chance, Joseph E. *Jefferson Davis's Mexican War Regiment.* Jackson: University Press of Mississippi, 1991.

Cutting, Elizabeth B. *Jefferson Davis, Political Soldier.* New York: Dodd, Mead and Co., 1930.

Davis, William C. *Jefferson Davis: The Man and His Hour.* New York: Harper-Collins Publishers, 1991.

Dodd, William E. *Jefferson Davis.* New York: Russell and Russell, 1966.

Eaton, Clement. *Jefferson Davis.* New York: Macmillan Co., 1977.

Gordon, Armstead C. *Jefferson Davis.* New York: Charles Scribner's Sons, 1918.

Langhein, Eric. *Jefferson Davis, Patriot.* New York: Vantage Press, 1962.

McElroy, Robert M. *Jefferson Davis: The Unreal and the Real.* New York: Harper & Bros., 1937.

Muldowny, John. "The Administration of Jefferson Davis as Secretary of War." Ph.D. dissertation, Yale University, 1959.

The Papers of Jefferson Davis. 7 vols. to date. Baton Rouge: Louisiana State University Press, 1971–1991.

Roland, Dunbar. *Jefferson Davis, Constitutionalist: His Letters, Papers, and Speeches.* 10 vols. Jackson: Mississippi Department of Archives and History, 1923.

Strode, Hudson. *Jefferson Davis: American Patriot.* 4 vols. New York: Harcourt Brace Jovanovich, Inc., 1955.

Winston, Robert W. *High Stakes and Hair Trigger: The Life of Jefferson Davis.* New York: Henry Holt and Co., 1930.

Dearborn, Henry

Brown, Lloyd A., and Peckham, Howard H. *Revolutionary War Journal of Henry Dearborn.* Chicago: The Caxton Club, 1939; and New York: Da Capo Press, 1971.

Erney, Richard A. "The Public Life of Henry Dearborn." Ph.D. dissertation, Columbia University, 1957.

Dickinson, Jacob McGavock

The Jacob McGavock Dickinson Papers. Nashville: Tennessee State Library and Archives, 1959.

Elkins, Stephen Benton

Lambert, Oscar D. *Stephen Benton Elkins.* Pittsburgh: University of Pittsburgh Press, 1955.

Endicott, William Crowninshield

Choate, Joseph H. *Memoir of William Crowninshield Endicott.* Cambridge: J. Wilson and Son, 1904.

Lawrence, William. *William Crowninshield Endicott.* Boston: Merrymount Press, 1936.

Eustis, William

Barnaby, James. *A Sermon Delivered at Salisbury, Mass., on the Death of His Excellency William Eustis, February 13, 1825.* Newburyport: W. and J. Gilman, 1825.

Fuchs, Emil

Fuchs, Emil. *With Pencil, Brush, and Chisel: The Life of an Artist.* New York: G. P. Putnam's Sons, 1925.

Morgan, Myrtis. *The Work of Emil Fuchs.* New York: Read Printing Co., circa 1923.

The Work of Emil Fuchs, Illustrating Some of His Representative Paintings, Sculpture, Medals, and Studies. New York: Bartlett Orr Press, 1921.

Gates, Horatio

Nelson, Paul David. *General Horatio Gates: A Biography.* Baton Rouge: Louisiana State University Press, 1976.

Patterson, Samuel W. *Horatio Gates: Defender of American Liberties.* New York: Columbia University Press, 1941.

Grant, Ulysses Simpson

Grant, Ulysses S. *Personal Memoirs of U. S. Grant.* 2 vols. New York: Charles L. Webster Co., 1885–1886, and numerous later editions, including E. B. Long, ed. Cleveland: World Publishing Co., 1952.

Catton, Bruce. *U. S. Grant and the American Military Tradition.* Waltham: Little, Brown and Co., 1954.

Hesseltine, William B. *Ulysses S. Grant: Politician.* New York: Frederick Ungar Publishing Co., 1935.

Healy, George Peter Alexander

Healy, G. P. A. *Reminiscences of a Portrait Painter.* Chicago: A. C. McClurg and Co., 1894; and New York: Kennedy Graphics, 1970.

Healy, Mary. *Life of George P. A. Healy, by His Daughter, Mary.* Chicago: no publisher, 1913.

de Mare, Marie. *G. P. A. Healy, American Artist: An Intimate Chronicle of the Nineteenth Century.* New York: McKay, 1954.

Holt, Joseph

Bateman, Roger. "The Contribution of Joseph Holt to the Political Life of the United States." Ph.D. dissertation, Fordham University, 1958.

Huntington, Daniel

Cantor, Jay E. *Drawn From Life: Studies and Sketches by Frederick Church, Winslow Homer, and Daniel Huntington.* New York: American Federation of the Arts, circa 1972.

Memorial Exhibition of Works by the Late Daniel Huntington at the Century Association. New York: Irving Press, 1908.

Hurley, Patrick Jay

Buhite, Russell D. *Patrick J. Hurley and American Foreign Policy.* Ithaca: Cornell University Press, 1973.

La Moore, Parker. *"Pat" Hurley, the Story of an American.* New York: Brewer, Warren and Putnam, 1932.

Lohbeck, Don. *Patrick J. Hurley.* Chicago: Henry Regnery Co., 1956.

Hutchens, Frank Townsend

An Exhibition of Recent Paintings by Frank Townsend Hutchens. Indianapolis: The John Herron Art Institute, 1912.

Jarvis, John Wesley

Dickson, Harold E. *John Wesley Jarvis, American Painter.* New York: New York Historical Society, 1949.

Kinstler, Everett Raymond

Kinstler, Everett Raymond. *Painting Portraits.* New York: Watson Gupthill, 1971.

Knox, Henry

Brooks, Noah. *Henry Knox: A Soldier of the Revolution.* New York: G. P. Putnam's Sons, 1900, and Da Capo Press, 1974.

Callahan, North. *Henry Knox. General Washington's General.* New York: Rinehart, 1958.

Denzil, Justin F. *Champion of Liberty, Henry Knox.* New York: Julian Messner, 1969.

Drake, Francis S. *Life and Correspondence of Henry Knox.* Boston: S. G. Drake, 1873.

Le Clear, Thomas

Viele, Chase. *Four Artists of Mid-Nineteenth Century Buffalo.* [Includes Thomas Le Clear.] Cooperstown: No publisher, circa 1933.

Lincoln, Benjamin

Bowen, Francis. *Life of Benjamin Lincoln.* In *The Library of American Biography.* Edited by Jared Sparks. Vol. III, 1837.

Cavanagh, John Carroll. "The Military Career of Major General Benjamin Lincoln in the War of the American Revolution, 1775–1781." Ph.D. dissertation, Duke University, 1969.

Lincoln, Robert Todd

Goff, John S. *Robert Todd Lincoln: A Man in His Own Right.* Norman: University of Oklahoma Press, 1969.

McHenry, James

Brown, Frederick J. *A Sketch of the Life of Dr. James McHenry.* Baltimore: Maryland Historical Society, 1877.

Mattson-Bose, Martin H. "James McHenry, Secretary of War, 1789–1800." Ph.D. dissertation, University of Minnesota, 1965.

Steiner, Bernard. *The Life and Correspondence of James McHenry.* Cleveland: The Burrows Brothers Co., 1907.

Marcy, William Learned

Spencer, Ivor D. *The Victor and the Spoils: A Life of William L. Marcy.* Providence: Brown University Press, 1959.

Melchers, Julius Gari

Gari Melchers: A Memorial Exhibition of His Works. Richmond: Museum of Fine Arts, 1938.

Gari Melchers: Selections From the Mary Washington Collection. Fredericksburg: Mary Washington College, 1973.

Gari Melchers, Painter. New York: W. E. Ridge, 1928.

Quenzel, Carol Hunter. *Belmont: Gari Melchers Memorial Art Center.* Fredericksburg: Mary Washington College, 1960.

Monroe, James

Ammon, Harry. *James Monroe: The Quest for National Security.* New York: McGraw-Hill, 1971.

Cresson, William P. *James Monroe.* Hamden, Conn.: Archon Books, 1971.

Gershon, Noel B. *James Monroe: Hero of American Diplomacy.* Englewood Cliffs: Prentice-Hall, 1969.

Gilman, Daniel C. *James Monroe.* Boston: Houghton Mifflin Co., 1898; and New Rochelle, N. Y.: Arlington House, 1970.

Hamilton, Stanislaus M., ed. *The Writings of James Monroe.* 7 vols. New York: G. P. Putnam's Sons, 1898–1903, and AMS Press, 1969.

Monroe, James. *The Autobiography of James Monroe.* Edited by Stuart Brown. Syracuse: Syracuse University Press, 1959.

Morgan, George. *The Life of James Monroe.* New York: AMS Press, 1969.

Pickering, Timothy

Clarfield, Gerard H. *Timothy Pickering and American Diplomacy, 1795–1800.* Columbia: University of Missouri Press, 1969.

———. *Timothy Pickering and the American Republic.* Pittsburgh: University of Pittsburgh Press, 1980.

Pickering, Octavius, and Upham, Charles W. *The Life of Timothy Pickering.* 14 vols. Boston: Little, Brown and Co., 1867–1873.

Poinsett, Joel Roberts

Parton, Dorothy M. "The Diplomatic Career of Joel Roberts Poinsett (1779–1851)." Ph.D. dissertation, Catholic University, 1934.

Putnam, Herbert Everett. *Joel Roberts Poinsett: A Political Biography.* Washington: Mimeoform Press, 1935.

Rippy, J. Fred. *Joel R. Poinsett, Versatile American.* Durham: Duke University Press, 1935; and New York: Greenwood Press, 1968.

Stille, Charles J. *The Life and Service of Joel R. Poinsett.* Philadelphia: Reprinted from the Pennsylvania Magazine of History and Biography, 1888.

Porter, Peter Buel

Cozzens, Frederick S. *Colonel Peter A. Porter, A Memorial Delivered Before the Century in December 1864.* [Includes a sketch of the life of Col. Porter's father, Peter B. Porter.] New York: D. Van Nostrand, 1865.

Proctor, Redfield

Partridge, Frank C. *Redfield Proctor: His Public Life and Services.* Montpelier: Vermont Historical Society, 1915.

Ramsey, Alexander

Ryland, William J. *Alexander Ramsey: Frontier Politician.* Philadelphia: Harris and Partridge Co., 1941.

Rawlins, John Aaron

Wilson, James H. *The Life of John A. Rawlins, Major General of Volunteers and Secretary of War.* New York: Neale Publishing Co., 1916.

Root, Elihu

Jessup, Philip C. *Elihu Root.* 2 vols. New York: Dodd, Mead and Co., 1938; and Hamden, Conn.: Archon Books, 1964.

Leopold, Richard W. *Elihu Root and the Conservative Tradition.* Boston: Little, Brown and Co., 1954.

Schevill, William Valentine

Special Exhibition of Portraits by William V. Schevill. Cincinnati: Cincinnati Museum Press, 1914.

Schofield, John McAllister

Schofeld, John M. *Forty-six Years in the Army.* New York: The Century Co., 1897.

Scott, Hugh Lenox

Harper, James William. "Hugh Lenox Scott: Soldier-Diplomat, 1876–1917." Ph.D. dissertation, University of Virginia, 1968.

Scott, Hugh Lenox. *Some Memories of a Soldier.* New York: The Century Co., 1928.

Scott, Winfield

Barnes, James. *The Giant of Three Wars: A Life of General Winfield Scott.* New York: D. Appleton and Co., 1903.

Elliott, Charles Winslow. *Winfield Scott. The Soldier and the Man.* New York: Macmillan Co., 1937.

Scott, Winfield. *Memoirs of Lieut-General Scott, LLD., Written by Himself.* 2 vols. New York: Sheldon, 1864.

Sherman, William Tecumseh

Lewis, Lloyd. *Sherman—Fighting Prophet.* New York: Harcourt-Brace, 1932 and 1958.

Liddell Hart, B. H. *Sherman: Soldier, Realist, American.* New York: Praeger, 1958.

Sherman, William T. *Personal Memoirs of General W. T. Sherman.* 2 vols. New York: D. Appleton and Co., 1875; and Bloomington: Indiana University Press, 1957.

Stanton, Edwin McMasters

Flower, Frank A. *Edwin McMasters Stanton, the Autocrat of Rebellion, Emancipation, and Reconstruction.* Akron: Saalfield Publishing Co., 1905; and New York: AMS Press, 1973.

Gorham, George C. *Life and Public Service of Edwin M. Stanton.* 2 vols. Boston: Houghton Mifflin Co., 1899.

Pratt, Fletcher. *Stanton: Lincoln's Secretary of War.* New York: W. W. Norton, 1953; and Westport: Greenwood Press, 1970.

Thomas, Benjamin P., and Hyman, Harold M. *Stanton: The Life and Times of Lincoln's Secretary of War.* New York: Knopf, 1962.

Stimson, Henry Lewis

Current, Richard N. *Secretary Stimson: A Study in Statecraft.* New Brunswick: Rutgers University Press, 1954; and Hamden, Conn.: Archon Books, 1970.

Hodgson, Godfrey. *The Colonel: The Life and Wars of Henry Stimson, 1867–1950.* New York: Knopf, 1990.

Morison, Elting E. *Turmoil and Tradition: A Study of the Life and Times of Henry L. Stimson.* Boston: Houghton Mifflin Co., 1960.

Redmond, Kent C. "The Education of a Statesman: Henry L. Stimson, 1911–1928." Ph.D. dissertation, University of Southern California, 1954.

Stimson, Henry L., and Bundy, McGeorge. *On Active Service in Peace and War.* New York: Harper, 1917; and New York: Octagon Books, 1971.

Taft, Alphonso

Leonard, Lewis A. *Life of Alphonso Taft.* New York: Hawke Publishing Co., 1920.

Taft, William Howard

Anderson, Judith Icke. *William Howard Taft: An Intimate History.* New York: Norton, 1981.

Cotton, Edward H. *William Howard Taft: A Character Study.* Boston: The Beacon Press, 1932.

Davis, Oscar King. *William Howard Taft, the Man of the Hour.* Philadelphia: P. W. Ziegler Co., 1908.

Duffy, Herbert S. *William Howard Taft.* New York: Minton, Balch and Co., 1930.

Dunn, Robert Lee. *William Howard Taft, American.* Boston: The Chapple Publishing Co., 1908.

Mason, Alpheus T. *William Howard Taft: Chief Justice.* New York: Simon and Schuster, 1965.

Pringle, Henry F. *The Life and Times of William Howard Taft.* 2 vols. New York: Farrar and Rinehart, 1939; and Hamden, Conn.: Archon Books, 1964.

Vance, Cyrus Roberts

McClellan, David S. *Cyrus Vance.* Totwa, N.J.: Rowman & Allanheld, 1985.

Weeks, John Wingate

Washburn, Charles G. *The Life of John W. Weeks.* Houghton Mifflin Co., 1928.

Weir, Robert Walter

Robert Weir: Artist and Teacher of West Point. West Point: Cadet Fine Arts Forum, 1976.

Weir, Irene. *Robert W. Weir, Artist.* New York: Doubleday, 1947.

Wilkins, William

Liscombe, R. W. *William Wilkins, 1778–1839.* New York: Cambridge University Press, 1980.

Woodring, Harry Hines

McFarland, Keith D. *Harry H. Woodring: A Political Biography.* Lawrence: University Press of Kansas. 1975.

☆ U.S. GOVERNMENT PRINTING OFFICE: 1992 320–497

PIN : 051306-